100 BEACHES
OF A LIFETIME

100 BEACHES
OF A LIFETIME
The World's Ultimate Shorelines

FREDA MOON & ASHLEY HARRELL

FOREWORD BY RAY COLLINS

NATIONAL GEOGRAPHIC

WASHINGTON, D.C.

CONTENTS

PAGES 2-3: Leuchtturm List-Ost, one of the oldest cast-iron lighthouses in Germany, stands amid the dunes on the island of Sylt (page 216).

OPPOSITE: Kayakers and beachgoers enjoy the cool blue water of Calanque d'en Vau (page 208), a cove in France's majestic Parc National des Calanques.

FOREWORD

Some of my earliest memories are of being on my mom's back underwater, my hands on her shoulders as we glided weightlessly through crystal clear water. Each time she surfaced for air and checked on me, I would, with slightly stinging eyes, eagerly tell her I wanted to go back under. I can still vividly recall the feeling of entering another world.

Forty years later, that feeling of weightlessness and floating through the waves remains.

Growing up in a single-parent household, I feel the ocean helped raise me, giving my mother a helping hand. The beach was at times a second parent, babysitter, best friend, and teacher; a classroom and playground that has been the single constant throughout my life.

Time and time again I've turned to its pure energy for cleansing and healing. I float in it to think. I submerge with clouded thoughts and reemerge with clarity. I ride its waves and celebrate. If I get a chance to watch the sun rise or set over the horizon as a bookend to my day, life is pretty darn good.

The ocean taught me patience; to sit back and observe before rushing in. What you initially see from land is just a snapshot, a fraction of the whole story. Often, there are larger cycles and longer patterns of set waves that aren't immediately obvious. When conditions are challenging, it's better to be still and observe to understand the whole picture, rather than focusing on the danger you feel surrounded by.

The ocean taught me humility. I've lost count of the times I've come in from surfing, battered, bruised, and bleeding from trying to impose my will on something so grand and powerful. Mother Nature cannot be contained

or controlled by humans. Although simple, it's certainly not easy to relinquish one's ego and become one with the ephemeral rhythm and flow of water.

It taught me respect. The more I understand the connection to something far bigger than myself, the more I fear its vastness, power, and significance.

These values have shaped who I am—both as an artist and as a human being—and the lessons I continue to learn from the sea and its shoreline extend far beyond the waves in which I play and work.

When researching waves to document through my photography, I constantly ponder the fact that storms from thousands of miles away generate swells that traverse entire oceans, ultimately concluding their journey at the beach, many of which are captured within this book. When we

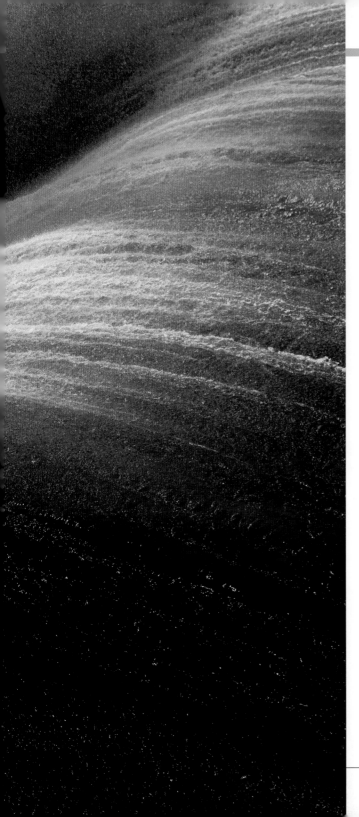

visit a beach, whether we're aware of it or not, we are experiencing the swell's final moments of a long voyage—sometimes from the other end of the globe—and its dissipation of raw energy. A part of that energy remains with us—a sensation surfers refer to as "stoke."

Each beach in this book has unique characteristics that warrant its inclusion. An exceptional set of contributing geographical factors make us drawn to it. I think part of the reason we are drawn to the ocean and its beaches—just like the pull of the tides—is that we are composed of more than 60 percent water. It is inside of us. Whenever we are near the water, wherever we are in the world, we are home.

When trying to adequately grasp what makes the ocean our home, I always come back to this quote by American author Christopher Paolini:

> *"The sea is emotion incarnate. It loves, hates, and weeps. It defies all attempts to capture it with words and rejects all shackles. No matter what you say about it, there is always that which you can't."*

—Ray Collins
Award-winning National Geographic photographer and author of Found at Sea *and* Water & Light

INTRODUCTION

I n late 2012, we were walking together along an isolated, nameless beach on Little Corn Island, located about 45 miles (72 km) off the Caribbean coast of Nicaragua. Shallow water lapped the shore and coconut palms cast long shadows over vanilla-colored sand. It was a long way from the Manhattan high-rise where, seven years prior, we had first crossed paths in graduate school. In the years that followed, we'd both become travel writers with a special fondness for Latin America. That walk along the Nicaraguan beach was the beginning of a friendship that stretched over decades and across the Americas.

All these years later, working together on this book, we can't help but marvel at the connective power of beaches. There's something magical about spending carefree time lying on the sand, strolling along the shore, wading into the water, and jumping the frothy waves. In those moments, we can all be our most present, playful, and childlike selves. We can come to know each other and ourselves in new ways. This book is a celebration of that power, as experienced through the world's most awe-inspiring and transformative beaches.

As if we were training to write this book, both of us grew up near beaches and have spent our careers visiting the very best of them.

For Freda Moon, who grew up in a rural coastal community in Northern California, the beaches of Mendocino County—which she still maintains are among the most beautiful stretches of coastline on the planet—were her backyard and playground. These beaches were where her mom cooked garlicky shrimp over a fire on warm nights and where Freda and her brother surfed, caught Dungeness crabs at river mouths, hunted for mussels on the

Ashley Harrell exploring a beach on Nicaragua's Little Corn Island, with photo taken by Freda Moon

rocks, and built elaborate forts out of driftwood. Because that remote, stunningly gorgeous coast was so familiar, it was easy to take for granted. As Freda got older and started to look out at the world, she gravitated toward cities—places of culture that were dynamic and varied. But her appreciation for beaches only grew.

For Freda, beaches came to represent not only places to experience and appreciate nature, but also areas where different kinds of people interact, subcultures mingle, and regional food is adapted and savored on the sand. These are places where religious practices—the cleansing of sins, baptisms, burials, and festivals—are held, new sports are born, musical genres are inspired, and art is created *en plein air*.

Still a country mouse at heart, Freda takes great comfort and joy in visiting remote beaches. But she's equally attracted to the kitschy Americana found

> *"The more beaches I have seen, the more I want to see."*
> —ASHLEY HARRELL

at a century-old beach boardwalk with a rickety wooden roller coaster, the smell of fried food and sweet treats mixing with salt air, shrieking kids, and couples canoodling on the sand.

Ashley Harrell grew up on the opposite coast of the United States, in a South Florida beach community just a coconut's toss from the Atlantic Ocean. She occasionally skipped school to hang out on Fort Lauderdale Beach—a notorious party spot featured in the 1960s spring break film *Where the Boys Are*—and enjoyed climbing into lifeguard towers late at night to listen to the waves and look up at the stars. At age 14, Ashley got certified to scuba dive with her dad, and eventually decided that she liked spending time around coral reefs and wilderness beaches instead of at beach bars.

In 2012, Ashley moved to Costa Rica and lived on the country's Pacific and Caribbean coasts, where she learned to surf. In 2015, she became a travel guidebook author and gravitated toward projects involving far-flung coastlines and world-class scuba diving. In the name of research, she's hiked California's 25-mile (40 km) Lost Coast Trail, visited Hawaii's volcanic green-sand beach (page 120), and explored Indonesia's colorful and biodiverse coral reefs off the secluded islands of Raja Ampat.

While *100 Beaches of a Lifetime* might suggest these are the world's "best" beaches, any true beach lover knows there is no such thing. An avid surfer and a family with young kids may be drawn to different coastlines, while a cultured cosmopolitan and a wilderness adventurer may each find beauty in their own stretches of shoreline.

We don't intend to create a bucket list with this book. Instead, we aim to capture the breadth of what a beach can be—from iconic beaches, such as Australia's Bondi (page 364) or Brazil's Ipanema (page 168), to inland beaches found in landlocked places, such as Lake Malawi (page 270). We also explore

Moss-covered rocks line the craggy coast of Northern California's Trinidad Bay.

ABOVE: St. Andrew's Bay is home to king penguins and elephant seals, which can grow to weigh as much as 4,400 pounds (1,995 kg).

OPPOSITE: At Florida's Fort Lauderdale Beach, a wavy white wall separates the often-bustling promenade from the sugary sand.

beaches with deep, complex histories and traditions, such as Traeth Mwnt in Wales (page 192), and places with endemic species and untamed nature (see South Georgia's St. Andrews Bay on page 146). Together, the one hundred locations covered in this book celebrate the expansiveness of beaches—in all their varieties—from around the world.

We hope it inspires you to go to a beach you've never visited, and maybe bring along a person (or people) you adore.

WHAT'S
A BEACH?

When we find ourselves lying on a towel in the sand, basking in the warmth of the sun, and taking in the sound of lapping waves, we have little choice but to relax and disengage. Perhaps that's why we rarely think to ask the simple question: What is a beach? In the simplest of terms, a beach can be described as a landform at the edge of a body of water—be it an ocean, a lake, or a river. That land might be covered by many things, but most commonly, those things are sand, pebbles, rocks, or seashells.

In addition, there's almost always some kind of erosion or weathering happening where the land and water meet. Water, wind, or both are continuously breaking stuff into little pieces, which in turn become part of the beach. This process is visible in places like the Grand Canyon, in Arizona, where the Colorado River chips away at canyon walls, and along England's east coast, where massive waves batter the cliffs. Other particles on a beach may have traveled a long way, carried by currents and tides, which may just as easily take them away again. As the renowned marine biologist, writer, and conservationist Rachel Carson once put it: "In every curving beach, in every grain of sand, there is a story of the earth."

Beaches are therefore ever-changing—you can never visit the same beach twice. They can be altered drastically from one season to the next by wind, waves, storms, and a shifting supply of sand. Beaches in winter often become narrower and steeper due to the destructive forces that cause erosion. In summer, calmer waves tend to bring sediment back to the shore, causing beaches to widen and develop gentler slopes.

No matter their shape, their body of water, or the power of their waves,

beaches provide an escape. However, that reprieve comes in many forms, depending on their locations and type of land cover. For example, the sand on Antarctica's Cuverville Beach is covered in ice and inhabited by penguins (page 186). The tropical Cook Island beaches are covered in sand and swaying coconut palms. Some Florida beaches have sand as white as powdered sugar from the ground quartz that made them, while California's Lost Coast is layered with pebbles that have been rounded by the surf. A few beaches are covered with sea glass, such as Fort Bragg in Northern California. And in places where the desert meets the sea, such as Namibia's Skeleton Coast (page 276), a beach may be totally barren.

Just about anything can get tossed around, washed up, or dropped off at a beach. If you were to lie on your towel at the edge of the water, you too would become part of one.

A boat docks in the sunlit lagoon of Aitutaki, one of the Cook Islands in the South Pacific.

TYPES OF BEACHES

The broad categories below were created to help you more easily find the type of beach you want to visit. However, many beaches could easily fall into more than one category. For example, Anse Chastanet in St. Lucia (page 90) is categorized as "remote" but it could also be "nature" for its rainforest or "wildlife" for its abundant marine life. But we chose "remote" because it is difficult to get there by car.

A HISTORICAL: Sites of significant cultural moments, like Anakena Beach on Rapa Nui in Chile (page 140)

B WILDLIFE: Where one can spot animals in their natural habitats, like Butiama Beach in Tanzania (page 282)

C SPORT-CENTRIC: Places known more for their activities than the view, like Playa El Zonte in El Salvador (page 62)

D CULTURE: Spots with a unique claim to fame, such as annual festivals like the Carnival of Viareggio in Viareggio, Italy (page 202)

E UNUSUAL: Rare or odd shores, like Papakōlea Beach in Hawaii (page 120)

F NATURE: Unspoiled and dramatically beautiful, like Sand Beach in Acadia National Park, Maine (page 134)

G ICONIC: Visually unique and historically beloved beaches, like Bondi Beach in Australia (page 364)

H REMOTE: Far-flung destinations but worth the effort, like Anse Source d'Argent in Seychelles (page 292)

I LAKE, RIVER, AND WATERWAY: Some of the many beaches not on the ocean, like Praia da Ilha do Amor in Brazil (page 160)

PART ONE

NORTH & CENTRAL AMERICA

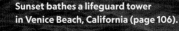

Sunset bathes a lifeguard tower in Venice Beach, California (page 106).

HOPKINS VILLAGE BEACH

This town beach is one of the centers of Garífuna culture.

CATEGORY: Culture   **BEST TIME TO GO:** January through March
WHAT YOU'LL EXPERIENCE: Belize Barrier Reef, West Indian manatees, Caribbean Sea

Although Belize was the last British colony in North America to gain independence (declared in 1981), the country's Garífuna population managed to maintain strong and distinct cultural traditions. The small 1,000-person village of Hopkins, in the Stann Creek District between Dangriga and Placencia, is considered by many to be the center of Belizean Garífuna culture.

The Garífuna—also known as Garínagu—are descended from Indigenous, Caribbean, and African groups, including the Kalinago-Taino (Carib-Arawak) people of present-day St. Vincent and the Grenadines. Driven from their homeland in the 18th century, the Garífuna first settled in Honduras, and eventually established communities in remote pockets in Belize and elsewhere along the Caribbean coast of Central America. The Garífuna's language, dance, and music were added to UNESCO's list of Intangible Cultural Heritage of Humanity in 2008.

The village of Hopkins has a beach that runs its entire length. Five miles (8 km) of golden sand and palm trees are peppered with unpretentious bars and restaurants selling local specialties including *hudut*—a stew made from plantains, coconut milk, and fish. By law, all of Belize's beaches are public within 60 feet (18 m) of the shoreline, making them easy for locals and visitors to access via roads and paths to the water that appear every few hundred feet.

OPPOSITE: Roland Williams (right) and Warren Martinez (left) are members of Hopkins's Lebeha Drumming Center, an integral part of Garífuna culture in Belize.

PAGES 24-25: Hopkins Village Beach is a short boat ride—8 to 10 miles (13 to 16 km)—from spectacular snorkeling in the Belize Barrier Reef.

> *"Drumming is so important to the culture ... Without drumming there would be no Garífuna."*
> —RONALD WILLIAMS, MEMBER OF LEBEHA DRUMMING CENTER

Along the mainland coast, the Caribbean Sea is not as consistently clear as it looks from the offshore islands. However, the mainland is an excellent jumping-off point for the Belize Barrier Reef System, which was designated as a UNESCO World Heritage site in 1996 and is just 8 to 10 miles (13 to 16 km), or about a half-hour boat ride, away. The reef system is the second largest in the world and, in 1842, Charles Darwin called it "the most remarkable reef in the West Indies." Among the endangered species that call it home are the West Indian manatee, several species of threatened sea turtles, and the American crocodile.

GARÍFUNA SETTLEMENT DAY

During the annual Garífuna Settlement Day, Hopkins Village celebrates the arrival of the Garífuna in Belize on November 19, 1802. The day is marked with a carnival-like spectacle of music and dance, drum ceremonies that can last all night, along with parades, prayers, and reenactments of the first Garífuna people's arrival by boat. Visitors can also learn more about the culture at the Gulisi Garifuna Museum in Dangriga.

1000 STEPS

A diver's paradise in the Caribbean with a marine reserve full of life

CATEGORY: **Nature**   BEST TIME TO GO: **December through April**
WHAT YOU'LL EXPERIENCE: **Sea turtles, eels, stingrays, barracuda, sheer cliffs, Caribbean Sea**

Some beaches aren't about the sun or the sand. At 1000 Steps, on the Dutch Caribbean island of Bonaire located about 50 miles (80 km) off the coast of Venezuela, it's all about what's beneath the water. In fact, the entire island is famous for easy-access scuba diving right from the beaches. And the entry point at 1000 Steps Beach is legendary among nearly a hundred shore dive sites on the island for its undersea life and iconic staircase.

Standing at the top of the stairs, which are cut into a limestone cliff, reveals one of the island's prettiest coastal views. There aren't actually 1,000 steps, but when you're walking down all 67 of them while carrying all your scuba gear, it certainly feels like it (and just imagine going back up!). Once you get down to the beach and wade into the surf, the visuals reach a whole new level.

Beneath the clear turquoise water, resident sea turtles, barracuda, and eels glide over a multihued coral reef system. When the sun is out, the full rainbow of colors really pops. Plus, the reef teems with life: Parrotfish munch on pieces of coral, while the branches of gorgonians oscillate in the current. Big-eyed squirrelfish hide among the staghorn coral and banded coral shrimp peek out from inside sponges.

The current isn't too strong here, making it suitable for divers of all skill levels, and snorkelers will appreciate the shallower areas. Divers can explore

These 67 steps cut into the tall limestone cliff descend to a pristine beach known both for its natural beauty and its world-class diving and snorkeling.

a drop-off just a few feet out that quickly reaches a maximum depth of 120 feet (40 m), and the visibility throughout is an outstanding 90 feet (30 m).

The dive site is within Bonaire National Marine Park, a UNESCO World Heritage site that stretches around the entire coastline of the island and extends to a depth of 200 feet (60 m). Established in 1979, the park is one of the world's oldest marine reserves.

You must purchase a Bonaire nature tag before exploring this site and the rest of the marine park. (Proceeds from the fee help to support park services and management.) You can access 1000 Steps from the Queens Highway. It's on the island's northern coast, about five miles (9.1 km) from Kralendijk. The access point is marked with a yellow painted stone. Park across the highway from the steps. If the descent seems too difficult, you can also visit 1000 Steps Beach from a snorkeling or diving boat.

NEARBY BEACHES

A SOROBON BEACH: Located on the eastern side of Bonaire near Lac Bay, this breezy beach offers shallow, turquoise waters and ideal conditions for windsurfing. Sorobon is dusted with white sand and bordered by mangroves.

B TE AMO BEACH: This secluded stretch of coastline near Bonaire's airport is popular with locals and visitors for its soft sand, calm waters, and delicious meals from the Kite City food truck. Top activities include swimming, snorkeling, and watching planes fly in and out of the airport.

C PINK BEACH: This remote pink-hued beach gets its color from crushed coral and shells mixed into the white sand. Amenities are limited, so make sure to bring your own picnic supplies, snorkel, and windsurfing gear.

PIG BEACH

A wildly popular white-sand beach where tourists swim with pigs

CATEGORY: **Unusual**   BEST TIME TO GO: **December through April**
WHAT YOU'LL EXPERIENCE: **Swimming pigs, clear water, other tourists, Caribbean Sea**

Tucked away in the Exumas, a collection of 365 wispy white-sand islands swirled in a painter's palette of blue-green sea, Pig Beach was the first—and remains the dreamiest—place to swim with pigs. How did this secluded, paradisiacal Bahamian beach become a swimming pig destination? Some locals say that pirates left pigs on Big Major Cay, thinking they'd use them for food later. Others claim the pigs were shipwreck survivors that swam to shore. The most likely explanation is that farmers brought a few pigs from Staniel Cay to the otherwise uninhabited Big Major Cay. Over time, the pigs learned to swim and paddled their way out to visiting boats for food. And it was adorable.

The beach was first popularized on *The Bachelor* in 2016. Soon after, pig-laden beaches started popping up on just about every major island in the Bahamas, including Eleuthera, Rose Island, Ship Channel Cay, and No Name Cay. But Big Major Cay is still the most famous.

In the Lynden Pindling International Airport in Nassau, the walls on the way to the baggage claim are adorned in giant photographs of—you guessed it—swimming pigs. The experience brings in tens of millions of dollars each year, and at this point it would not be a stretch to declare the pigs as the most popular attraction in the Bahamas. However, the unusual spectacle does come with some controversy.

Pigs are excellent swimmers and often take a dip when it is hot, as they don't have sweat glands to help them stay cool.

> *"The pigs are very tolerant of people.*
> *They decide what their relationship with*
> *the tourists will be, depending on how the*
> *tourists react to them."*
> —ROBIN SCHWARTZ, *NEW YORK TIMES*

In 2017, nearly a dozen pigs on Big Major Cay mysteriously died. An investigation found that sand ingestion during beach feedings was partially to blame. Additionally, videos of pigs nipping humans have made the rounds on social media, and animal rights advocates have accused tour operators of animal mistreatment and exploitation. There are also obvious health risks when pigs poop in the water where humans are swimming. In response to these setbacks and incidents, operators at Pig Beach have set strict rules for humane pig interactions. The swimming tours have remained as popular as ever, even attracting celebrities like Bella Hadid, Amy Schumer, Jennifer Lawrence, and Johnny Depp.

Some tourists spend up to $300 per person to fly round-trip from Nassau to Staniel Cay, where they board a boat for a half-day cruise around the Exumas. The stop at Pig Beach, a jaw-dropping powder-white sandy strip against crystal blue water, lasts less than an hour. After the visitors feed the swimming pigs and even jump in the water with them, some wade ashore and hang around with the pigs on the beach. Photographs of the pigs can be spotted along the walls of a nearby pavilion, with names like Ming, Shirley, Kenzo, Wolfe, Roosevelt, Milk Shake, Pebbles, Jon, and Dumpling inscribed below each one. There is also a rooster named Captain Hook. The whole lot of them appear healthy and happy, and their enthusiasm is often matched, if not exceeded, by the visitors themselves.

There is an average of 20 swimming pigs on Big Major Cay.

SWIMMING WITH OTHER FOUR-LEGGED FRIENDS

ABOVE: The famed "sea horses" that swim off the Indonesian island of Sumba

OPPOSITE: Piglets are a crowd favorite at Big Major Cay.

Riding a horse or a camel into the surf is downright magical, and there are a few places around the world where it's done well. On Noordhoek Beach in Cape Town, South Africa, you can saddle up and guide your horse into the crashing waves of the Atlantic, with Table Mountain soaring in the backdrop. As another option, on car-free Mackinac Island in Michigan, guided rides travel the scenic coastline to the edge of Lake Huron, one of the Great Lakes, where horses trot right into the water. At Umm Al Quwain Beach in the United Arab Emirates, travelers can ride camels along the shore and swim with them in the Persian Gulf.

To support the welfare of the horses and camels on your travels, choose reputable tour operators that prioritize animal care and provide proper training for riders. Respect any guidelines in place to protect the animals and their environment, which will ensure a responsible and enjoyable experience.

PLAYA PILAR

A beach named after Ernest Hemingway's beloved yacht

CATEGORY: Culture   BEST TIME TO GO: December through April
WHAT YOU'LL EXPERIENCE: Jardines del Rey archipelago, Buenavista Biosphere Reserve, Caribbean Sea

For decades after the 1952 Cuban Revolution, tourists were funneled into resorts at Cuba's most famous beach, Varadero, which was effectively off-limits to most locals. This divide between locals' beaches and tourist beaches has recently loosened, bringing new kinds of beach resorts, like Playa Pilar. Located on the country's northern coast, the beach is named after the writer Ernest Hemingway's cabin cruiser, *Pilar*, which famously plied the waters of the Jardines del Rey (or Gardens of the King) archipelago—now a biosphere reserve—in search of fish. Playa Pilar, in particular, was said to be among the literary giant's favorite spots in his adopted home, where he lived on and off for some 30 years and earned himself the nickname "Papa."

Until the 1990s, the archipelago where Playa Pilar is based—which includes the sister cays of Cayo Coco and its offshore islet Cayo Guillermo—remained undeveloped, despite having some of Cuba's most beautiful beaches. However, Playa Pilar, which has shallow water and powdery sand, is no longer untouched by development. A high-end boutique hotel opened in 2018 featuring over-the-water bungalows in 2019. Still, the beach remains unusually tranquil compared to the all-inclusive resort–backed beaches around Havana. It continues to be a popular location for deep-sea fishing, as well as snorkeling at the island's barrier reef, walking the sand dunes, sailing, and windsurfing.

Ernest Hemingway set his novel *The Old Man and the Sea* in the waters off Playa Pilar.

CAYOS COCHINOS

Find excellent snorkeling and seafood prepared by the Garífuna people.

CATEGORY: Culture   **BEST TIME TO GO:** February through September (dry season)
WHAT YOU'LL EXPERIENCE: Sea turtles, Mesoamerican Reef system, 13 coral cays, Caribbean Sea

The beaches on Honduras's biggest island, Roatán, are internationally known for both excellent diving offshore and the Caribbean-style party scene onshore. As another way to experience this spectacularly beautiful Central American country, the much smaller, harder-to-reach, and lesser-known Cayos Cochinos have fewer visitors and offer the opportunity to enjoy local Garífuna culture.

While technically part of the Roatán municipality, the Cayos Cochinos are both physically and culturally distinct from the rest of the Bay Islands archipelago. This tiny, carless island chain comprising two main islands and 13 coral cays is home to a community of Garífuna people. They practice sustainable fishing and subsistence farming on the mainland.

The islands are a national park managed by the Honduras Coral Reef Fund, which operates volunteer programs to remove invasive lionfish and protect the endangered hawksbill sea turtle. The fund operates a welcome center on Cayo Menor, which also coordinates dive trips to this protected area within the Mesoamerican Reef system.

Cayo Chachahuate is one of Cayos Cochinos' smaller cays, a crescent moon–shaped island only big enough for a couple dozen houses. Yet much of the Cochinos' population still lives on this sliver of an island, in stilted wood plank homes along the island's white-sand beach.

HISTORY

Cayos Cochinos translates to "Hog Islands," a name the islands received—if lore is to be believed—from the pirates who once frequented the area and left their pigs behind.

The sandy beaches found in the cays of Cayos Cochinos are ideal nesting grounds for the hawksbill turtle.

CHESTERMAN BEACH

Tofino's most popular beach is ideal for surfing and catching a dazzling sunset.

CATEGORY: Sport-centric　**BEST TIME TO GO:** June through August
WHAT YOU'LL EXPERIENCE: Tide pools, sandspit to a nearby islet, driftwood, Pacific Ocean

Canada doesn't usually come to mind as one of the world's greatest places to learn how to surf. But if you're willing to don a wet suit and travel to the tip of hauntingly gorgeous Vancouver Island, Chesterman Beach is pretty much a beginner's wave paradise. It's also a lot of other things, including a storm-watcher's destination, a wood-carving hub, a great spot to explore tide pools and sea caves, and a prime spot to watch the sunset.

Just a seven-minute drive south from the hippie surf town of Tofino, this white-sand beach is encircled by rock pools, wave-battered islets, and a temperate rainforest. And from early morning when the ethereal fog creeps over the beach, to sunset when the sky glows fiery orange, people are there to surf. Lots of them. While there are other great surf beaches in the area, Chesterman offers the most reliable breaks. Plenty of folks make their way over on two wheels, with their surfboards fastened to racks on the bikes.

The beach is split into two bays that are divided by what's known as a tombolo, or sandspit. During low tide, you can walk along the sandspit to neighboring Frank Island. The bays are referred to as Chesterman North and Chesterman South, and usually at least one of them has dependable, fun-size waves that novices adore. The waves in each bay benefit from winds that come from opposite directions, so generally, when the waves are too large

The surf on Chesterman South is generally mellower than Chesterman North, but both have dependable waves.

in one bay, the waves are just right in the other one. Occasionally, in summertime, the waves flatten out in both locations. Even for the most experienced surfers, a wet suit is required. The water temperature maxes out at 57°F (14°C) in August.

Regardless of the conditions, Chesterman is a hugely popular beach. In fact, people travel from all over the world to watch massive waves pummel the shore and crash over Frank Island during fitful winter storms. Perched on the northern end of the beach, the atmospheric Wickaninnish Inn even offers a "Storm Watchers Package" between November and March. The inn also contains a carving shed where local wood-carvers sculpt traditional canoes and other impressive works.

When the weather is calm and the tide is low, visitors wander across the sandspit to explore Frank Island, or creep around the tide pools at the northern end in search of kelp and shellfish like mussels. It is a great idea to bring binoculars to Chesterman, as waterbirds, orcas, and other marine life can often be spotted there. Meanwhile, nearby Pacific Rim National Park can be explored on kayak tours from the southern end of the beach.

Although Chesterman Beach is within the ancestral and unceded territory of the Tla-o-qui-aht First Nation, it is named after the white settler John Phillip Chesterman, who lived on the islet and tried to develop a copper and gold mine on a nearby island. For those willing to scramble over rocks or kayak south to Rosie Bay, there are some stunning basalt sea caves worth exploring. The caves were formed by waves crashing into large rocks over hundreds of thousands of years, eroding and hollowing them piece by piece. Mussels cling to the cracks and crevices, and other interesting creatures like sea stars and anemones can also be found in the caves. Some brave souls like to visit during low tide at night, when the reflection of the moon off the caves looks magical. Consult a tide chart and be sure to leave the cave before the water rushes back in, which can happen surprisingly fast.

There are two parking lots to access the beach—one on Chesterman Beach Road and another on Lynn Road. Both have bathroom facilities.

During low tide, visitors can walk to Frank Island from the north side of the sandspit. Those who do should keep an eye on the tide so they don't have to swim back.

ABOVE: Colorful sea stars cling to rock crevices during low tide.

OPPOSITE: A bird's-eye view of surfers in the waves off Chesterman

NEARBY BEACHES

COX BAY BEACH: Located just south of Chesterman Beach, this is where most local surf competitions are held. The tide pools and sea caves are also worth a visit.

MACKENZIE BEACH: A calm, family-friendly bay beach that's ideal for building sandcastles, exploring tide pools, and stand-up paddleboarding. It's not great for surfing, though.

LONG BEACH: Tucked into Pacific Rim National Park Reserve and spanning 10 miles (16 km), this extra-long beach draws surfers, storm-watchers, and driftwood enthusiasts.

LAKE ANNETTE

Wildlife is a big draw to this scenic lake beach in the Canadian Rockies.

CATEGORY: Lake, river, and waterway **BEST TIME TO GO:** June through September
WHAT YOU'LL EXPERIENCE: Elk, grizzly bears, eagles, Canadian Rockies, Lake Annette

This serene sliver of sand and sediment hugs the northeastern edge of Lake Annette—a spring-fed, glacial body of water within Jasper National Park, one of the Canadian Rockies' most spectacular outdoor destinations. The vaguely heart-shaped lake formed some 12,000 years ago at the end of the last ice age, when large chunks of glacier ice created depressions in the ground, called kettles, then melted within them.

Few people dare to go swimming in the chilly lake—on a warm summer day, the water temperature might hit 64°F (18°C)—but many visitors enjoy picnicking, grilling, and sunning themselves on the sand. Others have fun canoeing, kayaking, or hiking the wheelchair-friendly 1.5-mile (2.4 km) lake trail through the surrounding subalpine forest. The more adventurous lake goers can be found beneath the water's surface, decked out in scuba gear and exploring the depths of the 56-foot (17 m) lake. (Cold-water experience is a good idea, as are hoods and thick dry suits.) Divers can glide over a large, manufactured rock pile that teems with bottom-feeding fish.

However you decide to pass the time at this blue-green oasis surrounded by soaring mountaintops, keep an eye out for wildlife. Elk have been spotted taking lake baths, and the occasional grizzly bear family has been sighted in the picnic area. Give these animals plenty of space, and don't forget your bear spray.

NEARBY BEACHES

LAKE EDITH: Located down the road from Lake Annette, the beach is best visited in the late summer, when the water is warm enough to swim.

JASPER LAKE: While it's not technically on a lake but rather a portion of the Athabasca River, this narrow but long beach located northeast of downtown Jasper has stunning views of the Canadian Rockies.

Sunrise illuminates Majestic and Aquila Mountains, which are reflected in the calm waters of Lake Annette.

PLAYA BLANCA

White sand and abundant wildlife on Costa Rica's dreamy Caribbean coast

CATEGORY: Nature   BEST TIME TO GO: December through April
WHAT YOU'LL EXPERIENCE: Sloths, monkeys, rainforest, coral reefs, Caribbean Sea

For a wild slice of Costa Rica that feels frozen in time, look no further than Cahuita National Park on the country's less-explored Caribbean coast. The park encompasses 86 square miles (223 km²) of protected waters and a 3.9-square-mile (10 km²) peninsula covered in beaches and rainforest, both brimming with biodiversity. A thriving coral reef just offshore makes for excellent snorkeling, and a great launching point for exploration. The park's loveliest beach is a white-sand stunner called Playa Blanca.

The park is an easy walk from the village of Cahuita in Limón (population 4,000), which is defined by leaning coconut palms, unpaved side streets, and friendly locals who still converse in the local language, called Mekatelyu. The most common way to enjoy the park is with a hike starting from Playa Blanca at the southern end of town, next to the (now closed) Kelly Creek Hotel. Visitors sign in at the Playa Blanca entrance and are encouraged to donate $5 to help support park rangers and infrastructure before proceeding into the jungle, oftentimes accompanied by a wildlife guide to help spot critters.

Walk slowly along the first mile (1.6 km) between the entrance and Río Suárez, a stretch of water that follows Playa Blanca but also winds into the jungle. Visitors love to alternate between relaxing on the sugar-like sand while peering out at the turquoise waters and tiptoeing through the jungle, where playful monkeys, dangling sloths, brightly colored vipers, and wetland

OPPOSITE: Two- and three-toed sloths live in the jungle along the edge of Playa Blanca, but can sometimes be hard to spot in the dense foliage.

PAGES 50-51: While visiting Playa Blanca, visitors should also check out Cahuita National Park's other, more secluded beach, Puerto Vargas.

birds are regularly spotted. Just be sure to keep your bag in view: Clever raccoons and coatimundis have been known to poach unguarded snacks.

Those who prefer to snorkel off this gorgeous shoreline can meet a guide near the Playa Blanca entrance to grab gear, pay the entrance donation, and catch a 10-minute boat ride to the nearby reef. When the sun's out, the bright colors of the elkhorn, brain, and staghorn coral are on full display. And because the water isn't particularly deep, it's possible to dive down for a closer look at the swaying gorgonians and more than a hundred species of tropical fish. Eels, sharks, stingrays, and octopuses may also shimmy into view.

PROTECTING THE CORAL IN CAHUITA NATIONAL PARK

Established as a national monument in 1970, then upgraded in 1978, Cahuita was one of the first national parks in Costa Rica. The park was extremely popular with tourists until 1991, when an earthquake caused the water to recede by about 100 yards (91 m), destroying much of the coral due to sun and air exposure. Although the reef has recovered in some areas and tourism is again on the rise, new threats are rising due to sediments such as silt from nearby logging operations and fertilizers from nearby banana plantations. To keep the coral protected, snorkeling in the park is only allowed with a certified guide. You can also do your part by wearing reef-friendly sunscreen and staying off the coral.

PLAYA SAN JOSECITO

A quintessential jungle beach on the untamed Osa Peninsula

CATEGORY: **Nature**   BEST TIME TO GO: **December through April**
WHAT YOU'LL EXPERIENCE: **Scarlet macaws, monkeys, crocodiles, coastal hiking, Pacific Ocean**

Wilderness beaches abound on Costa Rica's jungle-shrouded and secluded Osa Peninsula. *National Geographic* magazine once called the peninsula "the most biologically intense place on Earth." And one of the most popular coves on the coastline of the famously biodiverse Corcovado National Park is the particularly untamed Playa San Josecito.

San Josecito is a 10-minute drive northwest from the Sirena Ranger Station at Corcovado National Park. With top-notch swimming, snorkeling, and coastal trails, this horseshoe-shaped, white-sand gem has rightfully earned its reputation as one of the peninsula's dreamiest beaches. Getting there—either by boat or on foot—is one of the best parts of the visit.

The beach lies about seven miles (11.2 km) southwest from Drake Bay, a remote local settlement surrounded by nature resorts that regularly send boats to San Josecito for snorkeling tours. The town also connects to the beach via a winding, 7.5-mile (12 km) road, as well as a narrow jungle footpath that hugs the coastline, meanders past scenic little bays, and teems with wildlife. This path is arguably one of the most awe-inspiring hikes in the country. (Please note: The trail is uneven, buggy, hot, and sometimes a bit difficult to navigate. If you are at all in doubt about your tropical hiking skills, hire a professional guide.)

OPPOSITE: **The Osa Peninsula is home to many beaches, including Playa San Josecito.**

PAGES 54-55: **Corcovado National Park is one of the last remaining habitats of endangered scarlet macaws.**

The hike starts with a hanging bridge over the aquamarine Agujitas River, where you can sometimes spot small crocodiles. After a couple of hours of walking, you'll approach the Claro River. At low tide, the crossing is easy on foot, but at high tide you'll need to be ferried across in a rowboat. Soon after, you'll reach the shore of Playa San Josecito, where you can finally plunk down to hydrate and eat some snacks. The beach is dotted with palms and almond trees, and you'll find scarlet macaws noshing on fruit or circling the area and squawking in pairs for much of the day.

After relaxing in the shade for a bit, you can take a swim. Rocky islets protect the beach and keep the waters calm and clear. The snorkeling is also top-notch due to vibrant coral and tropical fish. If you come by foot, rather than on a boat tour, consider packing your own snorkeling gear.

If you have a few more days to spare, continue your hike south to Corcovado National Park, where you'll likely spot monkeys and sloths in the treetops, and roam some other impressive wilderness beaches.

NEARBY BEACHES

PLAYA MADRIGAL: Entering Corcovado from the south, the trail follows this beach along the coastline, where you'll see a gold miners' cemetery along with rock formations and caverns at low tide.

PLAYA SIRENA: This scenic spot where the Sirena River meets the Pacific can only be reached by jungle trails. Rip currents and bull sharks make swimming here a bad idea.

OTTO BEACH

Spend lazy days lounging and snorkeling on this tiny Caribbean island.

CATEGORY: Remote   **BEST TIME TO GO:** August and September, January through May
WHAT YOU'LL EXPERIENCE: Creole culture, beach snorkeling, lobster dinners, Caribbean Sea

Fifty miles (80 km) from the mainland of Nicaragua, the Corn Islands are among the more challenging Caribbean paradises to reach. A speck of an island, Little Corn is even more remote than its nominally more developed sister, Big Corn, which at least has a single road and a tiny landing strip. Little Corn, on the other hand, is only accessible by boat from Big Corn, and its only town is nameless. Transportation is by foot, horse, or *panga* (a type of small fishing boat). And at low tide, much of the island's coastline is a narrow, sandy beach.

Though just two miles (3.2 km) long and a mile (1.6 km) at its widest, Little Corn has at least 12 named beaches. On an island full of inviting shorelines, Otto Beach, at the north end, is considered the most flawless. The beach is largely spared from the sargassum—massive patches of seaweed that wash ashore in heaping mounds—afflicting many western Caribbean beaches, including others on Little Corn.

Accessed via a 20-minute walk from the island's sole village, Otto Beach is said to be named for the patriarch of a prominent local family, "Mr. Otto," and to have some of the best beach snorkeling. Strap on your mask, snorkel, and fins beneath the shade of a palm tree and wade out into the sandy-bottomed water. Once you swim out past the seagrass, you'll find everything from barracuda to eagle rays swimming among an intact coral reef.

OPPOSITE: Otto Beach is one of a dozen beaches on Little Corn Island, which is also known for its lush jungles and pristine snorkeling.

PAGES 58–59: Fish served by locals on the beach was often caught that morning off the coast of Little Corn Island.

"How they came to be called the 'Corn Islands' is a mystery. Some say pirates and British buccaneers, who came here to restock supplies during the 17th and 18th centuries, misspelled the Spanish word for meat, 'carne.'"

—SCOTT HED, *INTERNATIONAL LIVING*

Other reefs on the island also offer the possibility of snorkeling with hammerhead sharks, though that's best done with a guide. Or you can take a day trip. From Little Corn, it's a two-hour panga ride to the almost entirely uninhabited island chain, the Pearl Cays, where endangered sea turtles can be seen nesting in August and September.

With only a scattering of small-scale accommodations, Little Corn is a pleasantly lazy place. Most days can be spent walking the dirt paths that lead to and from town through a mix of fruit orchards and jungles, listening to reggae or classic country music—an unexpected local favorite—at eclectic and artfully painted beach bars and restaurants, and drifting between a shady spot on the sand and floating in the warm, clear Caribbean waters. There are no large-scale hotels or resorts, but Otto Beach has the most upscale casitas on Little Corn, available for rent, with amenities like hot water and air conditioning.

ÎLE MOPION

A tiny sandbar where visitors act out deserted island fantasies

---

CATEGORY: **Remote**   BEST TIME TO GO: **February through April**
WHAT YOU'LL EXPERIENCE: **360-degree views, corals, not another soul, Caribbean Sea**

This might just be the smallest beach in the Caribbean. In fact, "beach" might be a generous term for this dreamy little sandbar. At just 100 feet (30 m) long—about the length of a basketball court—Île Mopion is devoid of development save for a single thatched umbrella hut. But this may also be the most desirable stretch of sand in the region. Its remote location 70 nautical miles (130 km) off St. Vincent means it is only accessible by boat and you're likely to have the island all to yourself.

Boaters take dinghies from nearby Union Island for a visit, and there are also water taxis and catamaran day trips that tour a series of islands including Mopion. If you're on a tour, beg the captain to visit if it's not among the scheduled stops; this is a once-in-a-lifetime island paradise. It conjures images from *The Blue Lagoon* and *Cast Away*. Even when the tides change, the iconic hut—which visitors carve messages into—is never fully submerged.

Not just a romantic day trip or ideal selfie backdrop, Mopion is also a snorkeler's paradise. The calm, clear turquoise waters are lovely for swimming and snorkeling. Beneath the surface are abundant corals and curious fish that swim right up to you. The most commonly spotted are queen and French angelfish, blue tangs, and banded butterfly fish.

HISTORY

For some unclear reason, this charming island was originally called Morpion, the French word for "pubic louse." The r was later dropped to sound more like Caribbean speech patterns.

A trip to this blink-and-you'll-miss-it island is a unique experience few will forget.

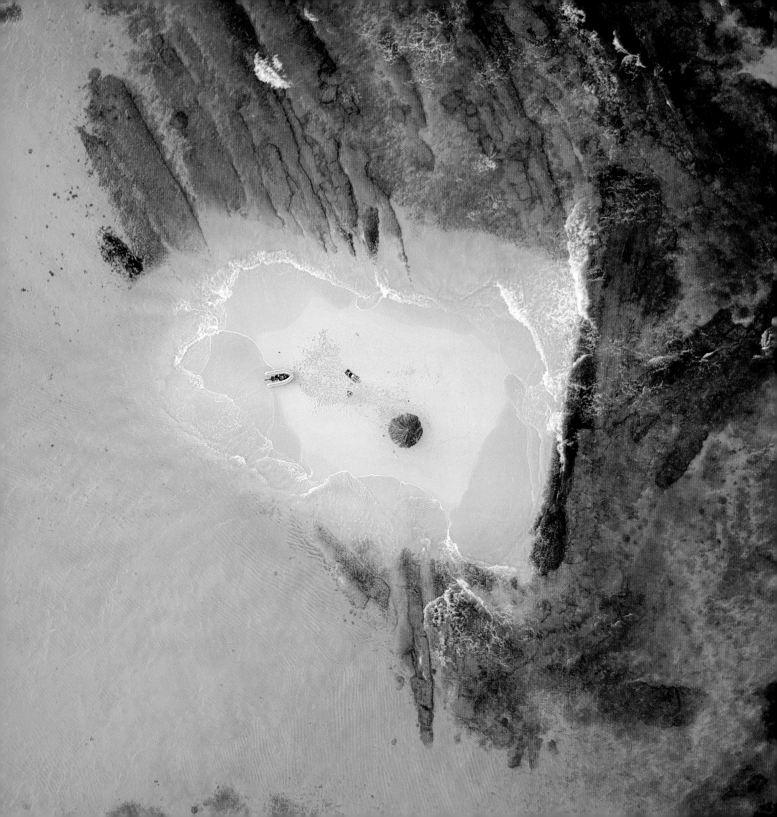

PLAYA EL ZONTE

A small Salvadoran surf town with an outsize global reputation

CATEGORY: Sport-centric   **BEST TIME TO GO:** Year-round
WHAT YOU'LL EXPERIENCE: Black-sand beach, volcanic peaks, Playa El Tunco, Pacific Ocean

On El Salvador's Pacific coast, El Zonte is among a handful of previously sleepy villages that have, in recent years, found themselves in the international spotlight as some of the world's greatest surf towns. Just 30 miles (48.5 km) from the capital of San Salvador, El Zonte is an adventurous surfer's dream. The town is uncrowded and affordable, with beaches that are blessed with a break for every level of wave rider, from novice to pro. The dry season (late November through April) has smaller, more beginner-friendly waves, while the rainy months (April through September) see larger breaks that are best for more advanced surfers.

Less well-known than the busy and cosmopolitan Playa El Tunco to the north, El Zonte is divided into two sections, which are separated by a river that flows from El Salvador's deep-green volcanic mountains. The river breaks the beach into the rocky eastern end, where surfers play, and the fine black sand of the west side, which is calmer and better for swimming.

While surfing may be this town's biggest draw for international visitors, El Zonte is known within El Salvador for something else. In 2019, the town became the first place in the country to adopt Bitcoin as its primary form of payment for everything, from necessities to snow cones. It was a big experiment in this poor country that earned the town the nickname "Bitcoin Beach" and led to the entire country adopting the currency in 2021.

El Zonte surfing is known for ultra-consistent swells and long right point breaks.

OTHER FAMOUS SURF BEACHES AROUND THE WORLD

International wave riders are constantly seeking out the best, least-crowded break.

A TEAHUPO'O, TAHITI, FRENCH POLYNESIA: Surf culture originated in Polynesia, where the sport has been practiced since as early as A.D. 400. Teahupo'o hosted the surfing portion of the 2024 Paris Summer Olympics.

B MAVERICKS BEACH, HALF MOON BAY, CALIFORNIA, U.S.A.: Since 1998, Mavericks Beach and its massive break has been home to one of the most famous big wave surf competitions in the world. From November through March, storms send swells ashore that can get as big as 60 feet (18 m) at their crest and regularly reach 25 feet (8 m) or more.

C HOSSEGOR, FRANCE: European surfing first caught on in Portugal in the 1920s, but it wasn't until American GIs began riding waves near Biarritz, France, after World War II that it became a genuine phenomenon on the continent. Today, the surf town Hossegor in the Bay of Biscay is one of the most famous wave destinations in the region, with pros regularly flocking to the break at La Gravière. La Sud is more welcoming to less-experienced surfers.

D ARUGAM BAY, SRI LANKA: Located on the Indian Ocean near Yala National Park—home to leopards and elephants along with an ancient Buddhist monastery—Arugam Bay's celebrated break draws surfers (and all-night partyers) from June through August.

E 'EHUKAI BEACH PARK, OAHU, HAWAII, U.S.A.: Probably the most famous surf beach in the world, most people refer to 'Ehukai Beach Park on Oahu's North Shore as the Banzai Pipeline (or simply the Pipeline). The Pipeline is actually the name of the beach's towering tube break, which forms over a shallow reef. It's not for amateurs. But 'Ehukai's shore is a fine place to watch the pros do their thing.

RESERVA DE LA BIÓSFERA SIAN KA'AN

An undeveloped coastline in one of Mexico's biggest nature reserves

CATEGORY: Remote   **BEST TIME TO GO:** November, February, March, and April   **WHAT YOU'LL EXPERIENCE:** Ancient mangroves, Mesoamerican Reef system, manatees, cenotes, sea turtles, Caribbean Sea

Sian Ka'an means "origin of the sky" in the Maya language. It's a fitting name for this magical, multicolored water world of mangroves, lagoons, wetlands, reefs, estuaries, cenotes (or sinkholes), sand dunes, islands, and miles of untamed beaches. This massive biosphere reserve is a UNESCO site of outstanding universal value, with both ecological and cultural significance to the Maya who traditionally inhabited it. For visitors, the reserve is a welcome reprieve from the heavily developed Riviera Maya to the north.

The 1.3 million acres (526,091 ha) of Sian Ka'an protects both coastal and marine ecosystems, including an increasingly rare sight in Mexico: undeveloped sandy beaches. That is due both to the area's protected status and the difficulty in accessing it. Visitors, usually arriving via guided tour, are astounded by the area's wild beauty. They must traverse a long, slow, bumpy road to arrive and often face an unpredictable sea. Accessing much of the reserve on one's own is difficult, requiring either a 4×4 or a boat to penetrate its single-track dirt roads and mangrove wetlands. The beaches here aren't well marked on maps or documented in online guides, but they are many, varied, and often relatively unvisited. The best way to find your ideal patch of sand is to drive until you find one that calls to you. Be sure to pack everything you need for a day at the beach ahead of time. There aren't many

OPPOSITE: There are miles of wild beaches along the coast of Sian Ka'an.

PAGES 68-69: A West Indian manatee swimming off the coast of Tulum can hold its breath for as long as 12 minutes.

> *"There is a great diversity of marine life, including the West Indian Manatee, four species of nesting marine turtles and hundreds of fish species."*
> —UNESCO WORLD HERITAGE CONVENTION

services available along the road to Punta Allen, a small Maya fishing community and the largest town within the biosphere reserve, at the end of the Boca Paila Peninsula. (As an environmentally fragile ecosystem, the park is critical for the region's fisheries.)

The reward of sitting on these secluded stretches of sand is worth the effort. In contrast to the beaches farther north, you're likely to have many places within Sian Ka'an to yourself—a luxury on this crowded but stunning coastline.

The range of species that calls the reserve home spans from large cats and land mammals, like jaguars and Central American tapirs, to marine mammals like West Indian manatees, to unusual endemic species like blind swamp eels that are only found within the park's limestone karst cenotes. The reserve is also home to the Muyil ruins, which are believed to have been built around 300 B.C.—earlier than other famous archaeological sites in the region, such as Chichén Itzá—and an ancient mangrove channel, built by the Maya more than 1,000 years ago as a trade route.

PLAYA DE LOS MUERTOS

A local beach tucked behind a colorful cemetery where families gather

**CATEGORY: Culture   BEST TIME TO GO: November 1–2 for Día de los Muertos; October, November, and May
WHAT YOU'LL EXPERIENCE: Devotional altars, fabulous food, protected swimming, Pacific Ocean**

Sayulita, found an hour outside of Puerto Vallarta on Mexico's Pacific coast, has a reputation as a party town and as a place where tourists flock for the region's powerful surf and lush, tropical landscape. Despite its popularity and proximity to the upscale resorts of neighboring Punta Mita, Sayulita retains its small-town characteristics. That means free-range chickens scurrying along beachside trails and colorful *papel picado*, or perforated paper flags, fluttering in the sea breeze.

A short walk over a steep hill from the town's compact center leads to Sayulita's historic cemetery, where locals gather to celebrate the centuries-old traditions of Día de los Muertos, or Day of the Dead. The graveyard, a mix of simple headstones, elaborate tombs, and colorful devotional altars terraced onto a hillside, is a striking and unusual site. The cemetery is also distinctive for its location: It directly borders one of Sayulita's most beautiful and beloved beaches, the aptly named Playa de Los Muertos.

Tucked behind the cemetery, the beach feels like something of a local secret. The small cove, which is well protected by rocky outcroppings on each side, has calmer water than the wider surfing beaches nearby, and it is frequented by multigenerational families. Servers from the modest beach bar rotate among the lounge chairs and sun umbrellas, plying skewers of barbecued shrimp, tropical cocktails, and cold beer. Be sure to pay your respects as you leave.

A beach vendor carries hammock chairs to sell on Los Muertos Beach.

PLAYA BALANDRA

An undeveloped mangrove-backed bay with multiple beaches and a mushroom rock

CATEGORY: Nature   **BEST TIME TO GO:** March and October
WHAT YOU'LL EXPERIENCE: El Hongo, stingrays, the Gulf of California UNESCO World Heritage site

Playa Balandra—located a half hour north of La Paz, the capital of Baja California Sur in Mexico—is an increasingly rare sight in a country with an inclination toward building megaresorts on its beaches. An immaculate, undeveloped beach, Balandra was designated a protected area in 2008 and became part of the massive Islands and Protected Areas of the Gulf of California UNESCO World Heritage list in 2012. This status has saved it from the fate of Los Cabos, located a two-and-a-half-hour drive to the south, which was little more than a fishing village until the 1970s and is now home to some 350,000 people, plus more than four million tourists a year.

As more visitors began to make their way north to the La Paz region in recent years, Balandra began to feel the crush of tourism. As a result, the Mexican government began implementing the kinds of restrictions seen at popular beaches elsewhere in the world. These included a modest and sporadically enforced admission fee and restrictions on the numbers of people allowed at a given time, with two shifts daily. The demand is so great that scammers urge tourists to buy special—entirely unnecessary—tickets in advance, so don't fall for those tricks.

Balandra is not a single beach, but a wide lagoon-like bay with multiple stretches of sand separated by small rocky peninsulas. At one such outcropping sits Balandra's often-photographed El Hongo—"the mushroom"—rock.

OPPOSITE: The beach is made up of multiple stretches of sand separated by small rocky peninsulas along Balandra Bay.

PAGES 74-75: El Hongo rock is one of the most distinctive formations on Playa Balandra.

"This is an adventure destination. We want people who want to explore, who want to preserve the environment the way it is, and to help us protect it."

—LUZ MARIA ZEPEDA, LA PAZ DIRECTOR OF TOURISM, *NEW YORK TIMES*

The top-heavy rock formation is said to have become a victim of its popularity. So many photo-happy visitors climbed atop it for a shot that it toppled in 1989. The iconic rock was reinforced in the 1990s, and then again in 2005 after it toppled due to heavy winds. Climbing on it is now prohibited.

Balandra's water is generally shallow, which means it's warmer than some of the nearby, less-sheltered beaches along this stretch of the Gulf of California coast, which can be a bit chilly to swim in during some parts of the year. While the water temperature here is lovely for a dip, locals advise shuffling one's feet in the sand as a precaution against encounters with stingrays, which are plentiful in the bay. As a nature preserve, the beach is almost entirely undeveloped and lacking bathroom services, though there is a scattering of *palapas*—thatched-roof shade structures—for free use and modest beachfront restaurants at nearby beaches.

PLAYA HONDA

A quiet, flower-filled island with a double-sided beach

CATEGORY: Historical   **BEST TIME TO GO:** January through April
WHAT YOU'LL EXPERIENCE: Panama Canal, Morro Island, sea glass, Paul Gauguin history, Pacific Ocean

This double-sided beach—Playa Honda on the eastern side, Playa Restinga to the west—is actually a sandspit. The landform comprising these beaches connects Isla Taboga, a small but historically significant (and dramatically beautiful) island in the Gulf of Panama, to the even smaller neighboring Morro Island. At high tide, much of the beach disappears beneath four feet (1.2 m) of water. But when it's exposed, this unusual beach has a striking view. It looks out at a crowd of supersize ships, each waiting its turn to travel through the Panama Canal. In the distance is the towering skyline of Panama City.

Isla Taboga, located just 12 miles (19 km) from the country's booming capital, is a day trip destination for locals who are shuttled back and forth on passenger ferries. The shallow Gulf of Panama is largely beachless, which makes Isla Taboga one of the closest places for the half million or so capital residents to lay a towel in the sand and swim in the ocean. On weekends and holidays during the day, vendors congregate along the path to the beach selling showy piña coladas served in emptied pineapple husks, topped with paper parasols. But when the last ferry of the night leaves, Taboga transforms. The island's only town, a 1,000-person village by the same name, borders the boardwalk and main dock. A colorful tangle of houses climbs Taboga's steep volcanic slope, where Iglesia de San Pedro—one of the oldest churches in

OPPOSITE: Taboga beaches have a unique view of the ships traveling to the Panama Canal's Balboa entrance.

PAGES 78-79: Hikers can make their way past the colorful houses of town to reach one of the island's highest points, Cerro Vigía or Cerro de La Cruz.

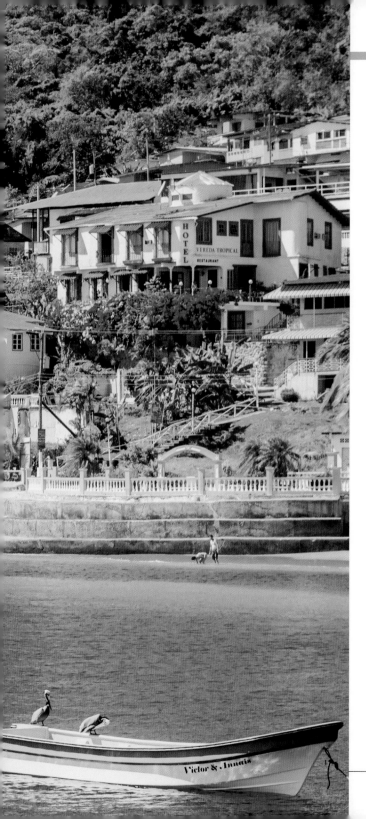

Latin America, built in 1524—sits at the center. At night, the roadless town is so quiet and calm that Panama City's bustle and concrete feel a world away.

Walking Taboga's promenade at dusk, the locals and few overnight tourists have the beach to themselves. Pangas (small fishing boats) are dragged ashore for the night, turning Playa Honda into a fleet parking lot and local hangout.

Considering its small size—about two miles (3.2 km) long and one mile (1.6 km) wide—Taboga has a deep and fascinating history. It was first documented by Europeans in 1513, when Vasco Núñez de Balboa visited it after becoming the first European to cross the Isthmus of Panama and reach the Pacific Ocean. In the 1880s, when the Panama Canal was in the early days of its construction, the French impressionist painter Paul Gauguin spent time at the island's malaria sanitarium—his first encounter with the Pacific tropics, which he would later capture in his most famous paintings. Because he was too ill to paint during his stay, there is no known artwork from his time on Taboga.

Beyond the shore, there's not much on Taboga but a colorful community and their brightly hued homes. Despite its proximity to one of the great cosmopolitan capitals of the Americas, the island feels separated from the capital. Yet the fleets of ships offshore are more than a spectacle. They're responsible for the inordinate amount of sea glass, essentially discarded glass bottles, that washes ashore here.

ÎLE RAT

A paradisiacal coral islet that's full of hidden history

CATEGORY: **Remote**   BEST TIME TO GO: **December through April**
WHAT YOU'LL EXPERIENCE: **White sand, bright turquoise water, palm trees, snorkeling, Caribbean Sea**

Natural disasters and political instability tend to dominate headlines about Haiti, so fewer people visit on vacation these days. Those who do will often arrive on the north coast aboard a cruise ship, and quickly realize that the island nation has some of the Caribbean's most attractive beaches. Case in point: Île Rat, a 3.7-acre (1.5 ha) coral islet, located just a 15-minute boat ride from Labadee.

When Christopher Columbus visited this tiny island oasis back in the 1400s, he called it Amiga Island, and the island's current owner—Royal Caribbean—still refers to it as such. Haitians, however, know it as Île Rat, or "Island of the Rat." The name is thought to refer to the island's small size, as it doesn't actually have any rats. The island does, however, feature a diminutive forest of coconut trees fringed by sugar-fine white sand that gives way to brilliant turquoise waters inhabited by corals and fish. Meanwhile, the surrounding bay (Baie de l'Acul) contains centuries-old cannons and anchors, and archaeologists have unearthed artifacts from ancient civilizations on the island itself.

Today, the mostly deserted island is equipped with sun loungers, a thatched-roof bar, and an outdoor grilling station, where local fishermen bring their catch. Visitors can choose from humongous crabs, lobsters, octopus, and a selection of local fish for the island chefs to prepare. The

OPPOSITE: **The Dragon's Breath Flight Line takes off 500 feet (152 m) above Labadee Beach and travels 2,600 feet (792 m) at speeds of 40 to 50 miles an hour (64 to 80 kph).**

PAGES 82-83: **Île Rat is so small that it only takes 10 minutes to walk around the perimeter.**

famous Haitian beer Prestige is consumed with abandon, as are rum cocktails on days when the cruise ships send passengers over from Labadee Beach, a veritable playground in its own right. Labadee features a water park, water sports like boating and parasailing, and an overwater zip line that's claimed to be the world's longest.

Non-cruising visitors arrive on Île Rat via a 15-minute scenic ride on a fishing boat from the Labadee water taxi areas. Local boat captains usually charge around $50 round-trip for two people, but rates should be negotiated in advance.

OTHER NOTABLE PRIVATE CRUISE LINE DESTINATIONS

GREAT STIRRUP CAY, BAHAMAS: Norwegian Cruise Line was the first to offer a private island for its passengers when it bought this former hideout for buccaneers lined with white-sand beaches in 1977.

OCEAN CAY MSC MARINE RESERVE, BAHAMAS: A former sand extraction site was transformed over four years by MSC Cruises into a low-key, environmentally rich oasis with a marine research center and numerous oceanside and lagoon-facing beaches.

HARVEST CAYE, BELIZE: A nature retreat jointly owned by Norwegian Cruise Line and the Belizean government, this island enables visitors to lounge on a seven-acre (2.8 ha) beach, snorkel in the Belize Barrier Reef, and learn about wildlife at naturalist Tony Garel's nature center.

FRENCHMAN'S COVE

This Jamaican beach is home to the world's first all-inclusive resort.

CATEGORY: Historical   **BEST TIME TO GO:** Mid-December through April (dry season)
WHAT YOU'LL EXPERIENCE: A natural lazy river, the Blue Mountains, Caribbean Sea

On the lush, less-developed northeast coast of Jamaica, near Port Antonio, is a small teardrop-shaped bay where an aquamarine river empties into the Caribbean. The beach at the river's mouth is called Frenchman's Cove. In the 1960s, the heir to a Canadian biscuit fortune developed what is thought to be one of the world's first all-inclusive resorts on said beach.

Garfield Weston, heir to his father's successful bread company and a biscuit tycoon in his own right, bought the 45-acre (18 ha) former sugar plantation as a personal retreat in 1956. But the property's deed required the land to be developed as a public resort, so Garfield enlisted his son, Grainger, to oversee the project.

The Westons hired a Texas-based architect named William Tamminga, who had worked on the Tryall Club in Montego Bay to design a so-called plantation community of luxury villas surrounding a Great House. While Tryall had been built around an existing historic home, Frenchman's Cove was effectively a blank slate.

Tamminga, an accomplished modernist, was inspired by the beauty of the Frenchman's Cove setting. He built a Great House with an expansive covered terrace, surrounded by 16 glass-and-limestone-faced villas nestled into the landscape.

OPPOSITE: **The swings over the river at Frenchman's Cove offer the ultimate photo op.**

PAGES 86-87: **Where the river meets the ocean lies the picture-perfect beach of Frenchman's Cove.**

The coastal Portland Parish is considered one of Jamaica's most beautiful regions, with the fertile Blue Mountains tumbling down to the coast, veined by rivers and thick with vegetation. Frenchman's Cove is a tidy little beach, so picture-perfect and immaculate that it looks like a secret hideaway.

But during its heyday, Frenchman's Cove and its eponymous resort were the opposite: They appeared on the big screen in movies like *Lord of the Flies* and *Knight and Day* and hosted a slew of visiting celebrities. Both Hollywood royalty—including mid-century icons such as Elizabeth Taylor, Richard Burton, Ian Fleming, and Errol Flynn—and actual royalty, including Queen Elizabeth II, have stayed there. During the period when it was among the most expensive and exclusive resorts in the world, it felt like a private paradise for those fortunate enough to visit.

Today, Frenchman's Cove is considerably more accessible. The resort's historic grounds—lush with greenery—and movie star-seducing beach are both open to the public. Anyone willing to pay the hotel's modest fee (currently less than $20) can rent a daybed and umbrella where queens and celebrities once lounged. The beach restaurant serves cocktails and a fried fish dish that locals rave about.

There are swings in areas above the river, where the cool mountain water meets the warm Caribbean, and along the bay's shore, where there are often gentle waves.

TRINIDAD AND TOBAGO

MARACAS BEACH

The perfect beach to wash away the excesses of Carnival

CATEGORY: Culture   **BEST TIME TO GO:** February or March, during Carnival
WHAT YOU'LL EXPERIENCE: Bake and shark, waterfalls, Trinidadian culture, Caribbean Sea

Trinidad and Tobago's annual Carnival, held on the days leading up to Ash Wednesday, is the island nation's biggest party. There are fetes (parties), soca (a musical style with African and East Indian influences), calypso and steel pan competitions, and a massive, colorful parade. Masqueraders fill the streets wearing feathers and beads while revelers shimmy and dance. The center of these raucous festivities is Port of Spain, the capital city. The post-revelry custom is to spend the day at the beach—specifically Maracas Bay, the island's most breathtaking stretch of sand—recovering from days of indulgence.

The half-hour drive to Maracas Bay winds through mountains and forests. The beach itself is surrounded by the same verdant hills, with ample hiking trails leading to nearby waterfalls. During weekends and holidays, Maracas can be busy. But the size of the wide bay means there's typically room for everyone. Waves along the semicircular bay average about three feet (1 m), making for good bodyboarding.

The long stretch of off-white sand and palms is lined with beach huts that serve the most celebrated of Trinidadian cuisine: bake and shark. Though this sandwich made of fried dough, shark meat, and distinctive sauce is often referred to as "street food," bake and shark is a quintessential beach eat, popularized right in Maracas.

Palm trees shade beachgoers enjoying the crystal clear waters off Maracas Beach.

ANSE CHASTANET

Volcanic sand and top-notch snorkeling at the foot of the famous Pitons

---

CATEGORY: Remote   **BEST TIME TO GO:** December through April
WHAT YOU'LL EXPERIENCE: Pitons, coral reefs, volcanic sand, hawksbill turtles, rainforest, Caribbean Sea

Arguably the best beach on St. Lucia for snorkeling and diving, Anse Chastanet is also a must-visit for the breathtaking rainforest views along the shoreline. And of course, for its iconic backdrop: the Pitons. The distinctive spires are part of a vast volcanic complex spanning more than 400 miles (644 km) along the Lesser Antilles.

Located in Soufrière on St. Lucia's southwest coast, the beach is secluded but sees significant crowds, given its status as one of the area's top romantic getaways. Anse Chastanet Beach is part of an eponymous luxury resort known for kind staff members and eco-friendly practices, including coral reef restoration projects. Hanging out at the beach is free to the public, but be warned: The roads to get there can be difficult to navigate. Oftentimes, visitors opt to arrive by water taxi instead.

The main draw on this beach is the undersea environment, where marine life is abundant. Boat tours regularly bring snorkelers here, but you're also welcome to plunge in directly from the shore. Four numbered snorkeling zones are accessible from the shore and feature colorful underwater scenes, including shallow fringing reefs and intriguing boulder formations populated with colorful (and sometimes enormous) sponges. Hard corals are sparse, but a soft coral garden thrives with fans, plumes, and rods.

Offshore, seagrass beds attract tropical fish, turtles, and rays. And despite

OPPOSITE: The volcanic spires of the Pitons are visible from the beach.

PAGES 92-93: These blue-striped grunts are just one of more than 100 species of fish found in the reefs off Anse Chastanet.

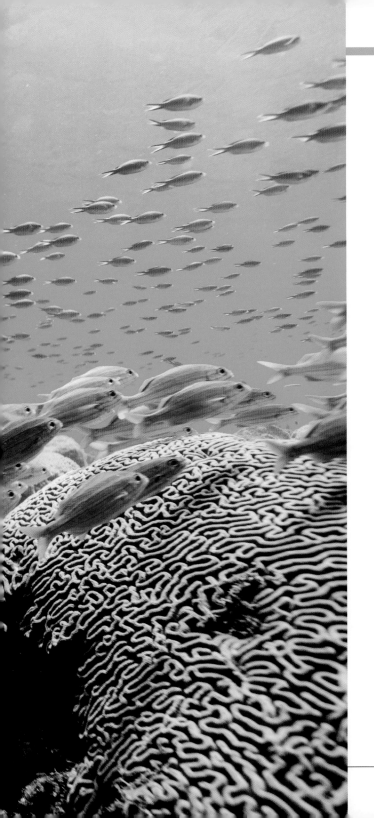

some areas showing coral decline and stressed sea fans, the Soufrière Marine Management Area, which protects the coast by Anse Chastanet, fosters healthy populations of squid, turtles, eels, lobsters, and unique species including the flying gurnard, a bottom-dweller with flared pectoral fins that resemble wings.

For divers with an interest in spotting nocturnal sea creatures, the local dive shop, Scuba St. Lucia, runs guided night adventures, where you might spot eels, octopuses, lobsters, and sleeping parrotfish. For those who prefer dry land, visit the beach between March and November, when you can see hawksbill nests. If you schedule your trip between May and October, you might be lucky enough to explore the beach alongside the hatchlings. (The St. Lucia government advises giving the turtles and their nests appropriate space during the nesting and hatching seasons.)

St. Lucia has long been the ultimate honeymoon destination for its seclusion, top-notch natural attractions, and relaxed vibe. The Kwéyòl village communities host nightly fish fries, and the island's heritage is represented in the local cuisine: a fusion of African, European, Indian, and Indigenous Caribbean influences. Other activities in the area range from jungle biking and boat tours to hiking the famous Pitons of Gros Piton and Tet Paul. Keep in mind: Treks to the top of the Pitons are notoriously brutal.

SLEEPING BEAR DUNES BEACHES

Where massive sand dunes meet the Great Lakes

CATEGORY: Lake, river, and waterway   **BEST TIME TO GO:** Year-round
WHAT YOU'LL EXPERIENCE: Geological history, ridgetop hiking trails, Lake Michigan

The sand at Sleeping Bear Dunes National Lakeshore rises more than 100 feet (30 m) overhead—a towering wave of beach descending to the blue waters of Lake Michigan. Formed by the same glaciers that created the Great Lakes, Sleeping Bear Dunes take its name from the Ojibwe peoples. According to the Ojibwe, who are part of the larger Anishinaabe peoples, one of the dunes was a mother bear who watched her cubs drown in the lake. Unable to save them, she planted herself on the shore in an eternal vigil. It's a story as striking as the national park is stunning.

This stretch of coastline, west of Traverse City, was defined by the Ice Age. During that period, when frozen water covered much of what is now the northern United States, river valleys were eroded, deepened, and widened by the weight and power of the flowing glaciers. The sediment created by this erosion as the last of the Ice Age glaciers retreated 11,800 years ago was deposited on the lakeshore by winds and waves.

Those ancient glaciers left enough sand, silt, and rock to create several distinct forms of dunes along Michigan's western coast. Beach dunes, like the ones found at Aral Dunes in Platte Bay, formed at lake level—entirely of sand and vegetation—and grew to 100 feet (30 m). Others developed on

In spring and summer, wildflowers, like this purple harebell, bloom along the paths lining the dunes.

> *"By strolling the beaches you may see another reminder of geological time, the 'Petoskey Stone.' A Petoskey is a fossil colonial coral. These corals lived in warm, shallow seas that covered Michigan during Devonian time, some 350 million years ago."*
>
> —SLEEPING BEAR DUNES VISITORS BUREAU

headland bluffs, which blocked the wind from carrying the sand any farther and created truly massive mounds, like Sleeping Bear Dunes, which reach some 460 feet (140 m) before falling to the beach below.

The most famous dune at Sleeping Bear isn't the tallest (that honor belongs to Empire Bluffs, at 450 feet [137 m] tall). Instead, it's the Dune Climb, a 284-foot-tall (87 m) wall of sand alongside the park's Glen Lakes. It is the most accessible and widely climbed of the dunes—considered a rite of passage for many midwestern kids. From the top of the Dune Climb, which marks the eastern edge of Sleeping Bear Plateau, many visitors opt to continue across the four-square-mile (10.4 km^2) dune system—a 1.7-mile (2.7 km) hike in each direction—to reach Lake Michigan and the dramatic sight of Sleeping Bear beach.

A year-round destination, sledding is allowed during winter months, while summer is best for camping (May 1 to October 15) and swimming. Spring and summer offer wildflowers, and fall brings colorful foliage. During July and August, the water off the beach typically stays above 68°F (20°C)—perfect for a refreshing freshwater swim. However, no lifeguards are on duty and visitors should be aware of rip currents. Other popular Sleeping Bear activities include boating and fishing, and, for hearty surfers, this stretch of Great Lakes shoreline even has rideable waves year-round, though appropriate gear is obviously necessary in the fall and winter.

The trail along Empire Bluff offers views of Lake Michigan and Sleeping Bear Dunes.

D

OTHER NOTABLE GREAT LAKES BEACHES

A INDIANA DUNES NATIONAL PARK, PORTER, INDIANA, U.S.A.: Just 50 miles (80.5 km) from Chicago is one of the newest—and most biodiverse—national parks in the United States (it was designated in 2020), with 20 miles (32.2 km) of shoreline and eight separate beaches to explore.

B BIG BAY STATE PARK, MADELINE ISLAND, WISCONSIN, U.S.A.: Part of the Apostle Islands National Lakeshore, this state park is—like the rest of the Apostles—only accessible from the mainland by boat. The park's 1.5-mile (2.4 km) beach is backed by a boardwalk and campground, a great base for exploring nearby sea caves by kayak.

C PARK POINT RECREATION AREA, DULUTH, MINNESOTA, U.S.A.: Notable as the world's longest freshwater sandbar, this narrow, seven-mile (11.3 km) spit of sand sits between Superior, Wisconsin, and the scenic college town of Duluth. When the wind blows from the northeast, kicking up waves, the beach is popular with Lake Superior surfers.

D SAUBLE BEACH, BRUCE PENINSULA, ONTARIO, CANADA: On the Canadian coast of Lake Huron, Sauble Beach is a 4.3-mile (7 km) stretch of white sand and shore grass where subsurface sandbars keep the water temperature warm and the surface calm. Located less than three hours from Toronto, it has long been one of Canada's most popular beach destinations and is known for its kitschy, retro vibe.

INKWELL BEACH

A historically Black beach in one of New England's most iconic destinations

CATEGORY: **Historical**   BEST TIME TO GO: **Spring (April, May) or fall (September, October)**
WHAT YOU'LL EXPERIENCE: **Pastel cottages, African American history, Atlantic Ocean**

No two sources seem to agree about when or how Inkwell Beach got its name. Some say it came from Martha's Vineyard's white residents, a moniker rooted in racism. Others say the name was always intended as a celebration, a nod to the Black writers and intellectuals who began frequenting Oak Bluffs' town beach in the early 20th century. Whatever its origin, Inkwell has endured as a point of pride for the island's Black beachgoers, many of whom return year after year, generation after generation, to this narrow sliver of sand beside the island's ferry terminal and overlooking the glittering Atlantic.

Martha's Vineyard, a 20-mile-long (32 km) island off the coast of Cape Cod, Massachusetts, has just 23,000 year-round residents. But during the summer, the Vineyard's population swells and its beaches, including Oak Bluffs' Inkwell, attract crowds from the Northeast and beyond.

A modest municipal beach, Inkwell is one of many historically Black beaches—places where Black bathers were allowed during the Jim Crow era, when most popular destinations were segregated—around the country. But unlike many others, including another well-known "Ink Well" beach in Los Angeles, Oak Bluffs has remained a beloved summer escape for Black elites.

Martha's Vineyard's northernmost village, Oak Bluffs, has attracted Black beachgoers since the 1800s, when the island became the hub of a

OPPOSITE: **The Polar Bears, a club founded in 1946 as a safe space for Black swimmers, meets up every morning in Oak Bluffs to exercise and have fun in the water.**

PAGES 102-103: **Inkwell Beach is positioned between two jetties, with a direct view of the ferry terminal.**

booming whaling trade and, later, a retreat for the Methodist Revival movement. The arrival of Black whalers, domestic workers, and Methodist worshippers eventually led to the establishment of the town's vibrant and uncommonly inclusive (for its time) tourism industry. In 1912, Charles and Henrietta Shearer opened Shearer Cottage, the first summer inn on Martha's Vineyard to welcome Black guests. The rest of the island didn't allow Black guests to stay in local accommodations until the 1960s.

Known as Cottage City until 1907, when it was reincorporated as Oak Bluffs, the town became famous for its pastel-hued gingerbread cottages—modestly sized vacation homes with outsize personality—and its reputation as a refuge from racism.

It's fitting, then, that when Barack Obama became the United States' first Black president, he made Martha's Vineyard his presidential summer home, spotlighting the island's long history of racial integration. The Obama family's ties to Oak Bluffs began earlier, in 2004, when Obama was a senator contemplating a run for the White House. He came at the invitation of a longtime friend and later senior advisor, Valerie Jarrett, who was among many prominent Black intellectuals, writers, academics, and civil rights leaders with a history in the area.

BOWMAN'S BEACH

A barrier island beach best known for seashell hunting

CATEGORY: Unusual   **BEST TIME TO GO: December through April**
WHAT YOU'LL EXPERIENCE: Beachcombers, seashell museum, Gulf of Mexico

Bowman's Beach on Sanibel Island is an undeveloped stretch of sand carpeted with shells: false angel wings, coquinas, conchs, whelks, junonias, cockles, sand dollars, and banded tulips, to name a few. A quarter-mile (400 m) walk from the road gives the beach a hidden feel, but among beachcombers, it's famous. Considered one of the best shelling shores in the country, Bowman's is the beneficiary of its geography, as an underwater shelf scoops the shells of gastropods and bivalves onto the shore like a special delivery from the ocean gods themselves.

Sanibel and its sister island, Captiva, are curved barrier islands just off Fort Myers, Florida, in the Gulf of Mexico. Storms and sea currents roll through the area, depositing a quantity and variety of seashells—hundreds of species, sometimes several feet deep—found in few other places on Earth. Indeed, the beach attracts so many shell enthusiasts, nearby hotels offer specially equipped sinks and tables for handling these delicate castoffs.

Located mid-island, Bowman's is arguably the best of Sanibel's shelling beaches, but it's far from the only one. In the early dawn, you'll find the area's most devoted beachcombers with flashlights in hand, bent in a crouched position—the so-called sanibel stoop—fingers needling the water's edge. If you're fortunate enough to visit Sanibel and spot one of its prized souvenirs, don't be surprised to find yourself doing the stoop as well.

Sunset warms the shells that carpet Bowman's Beach.

VENICE BEACH

This SoCal beach is renowned for its street and surf cultures.

CATEGORY: Iconic   **BEST TIME TO GO:** Year-round
WHAT YOU'LL EXPERIENCE: Weight lifters, offbeat boardwalk performers, skateboarders, Pacific Ocean

Ask most people how they might imagine Southern California, and they're likely to describe Venice Beach. With its colorful, bohemian, palm tree–lined boardwalk, this coastal enclave of greater Los Angeles is home to one of the country's most iconic beach cultures. Venice's two-mile (3.2 km) coastline of tan sand is dotted with rainbow-painted lifeguard shacks and packed with people.

It's a flamboyant, eccentric, and sometimes raunchy scene. It's also a place where L.A.'s theatrics are on full display: One walk along the boardwalk and you'll see a spectacle of street performers, scantily clad bodybuilders, skateboarders doing kickflips, families hooking fish on the pier, drum circles, in-line skaters dancing on wheels, and plenty of nods to alternative lifestyles and unconventional behavior of all kinds.

Venice Beach spans the entire waterfront of one of Los Angeles's most famous neighborhoods. The beach, which now draws some 30,000 people a day, is as pleasant a place as anywhere to sunbathe or splash in the cool Pacific (wet suits should be worn for longer dips in the ocean). But its real charm lies in its circus-like atmosphere—its sword-swallowers and fire breathers, its oddball characters, and West Coast cultural trendsetters.

Among the subcultures that found their footing along Venice's boardwalk is the bodybuilding movement that had its heyday here in the 1970s and '80s.

Weight lifters and body-builders flock to the Muscle Beach Venice outdoor gym to work out and be seen.

> *"When you did your chin-ups, your presses, your curls, you got the tan everywhere. Then we would run over to the ocean [and] jump into the waves."*
>
> —ARNOLD SCHWARZENEGGER, ACTOR, POLITICIAN, AND FORMER MR. UNIVERSE

Arnold Schwarzenegger, Lou Ferrigno (the original Incredible Hulk), and many others sculpted their physiques at an outdoor weight lifting and gymnastics center at Venice that was dubbed Muscle Beach. Later depicted in the classic 1977 documentary *Pumping Iron*, the original Muscle Beach was founded in 1934 in Santa Monica and eventually relocated from that increasingly affluent neighborhood to the grittier Venice in the 1950s.

In its early days, Muscle Beach was the home of "physical culture," which emphasized healthy eating and gymnastics. It was a wholesome place, where acrobats tossed each other through the air, impressing onlookers with their somersaults and uncommonly tanned and toned bodies. Later, Muscle Beach evolved into a steroid- and celebrity-centered scene, emblematic of Los Angeles's appearance-centric reputation.

During its relatively short life, Venice Beach has had a wild ride. It was the creation of Abbot Kinney, a wealthy—and visionary—tobacco magnate who was educated in Europe and dreamed of creating an American version of his favorite Italian city. In 1904, Kinney won a piece of oceanside marshland, then called Ocean Park, in a coin toss and decided to build a Venice-themed amusement park and planned community along the Pacific. His project showcased Venetian-style canals and Renaissance-era intellectualism. Along with its swimming pools, roller coasters, and gondolas, "Venice of America" had a 3,500-person auditorium that hosted lectures by visiting academics. Kinney's vision was a success. In just over a decade, a swamp was transformed into a tourist destination. When Kinney died in 1920, Venice was incorporated by Los Angeles, a growing city under the sway of technological progress. All but a handful of Kinney's canals were filled to make room for roads and cars.

Abbot Kinney's canal system was originally 16 miles (26 km) long, but only six canals remain today.

ABOVE: Skaters line the concrete Venice Beach Skate Park, which opened in 2009 on Ocean Front Walk.

OPPOSITE: Sunset illuminates the graffiti that covers not only the walls but also the trunks of the palm trees.

Then, in the early days of the Great Depression, oil was discovered on the Venice Peninsula. What had been an oceanside playground became an industrial landscape of mechanical derricks, and Venice's beach was blackened by crude.

California is famous for reinventing itself, and Venice's oil boom led to a new era of mid-century prosperity in the 1960s. With it came a breezy beach culture of bikinis, surf rock, the *Gidget* films, and *Beach Blanket Bingo*. But the area's personalities were always just below the surface, waiting for their debut on the boardwalk stage. From its thriving LGBTQIA+ community to its embrace of California's mind-altering cash crop of cannabis, Venice always seems to be on the cutting edge of the counterculture.

URBAN BEACHES

These sandy shores prove that some of the best beaches can be found within city limits.

Most of the world's greatest cities are defined by their memorable skylines, significant industries, or distinctive architecture. But a smaller number are best known for their waterfronts. These famed beach cities have iconic promenades, like the squiggly lined sidewalk of Copacabana in Rio de Janeiro, Brazil, or notable attractions like the Bondi Icebergs pool in Sydney, Australia.

A city built for its sand and sea is a sort of resort town on steroids. What these leisure lands lack in tranquility and unspoiled nature, they make up for in culture, fascinating histories, and the benefit of being an escape from the city and an extension of urban life.

Centuries before it became a bustling resort zone within greater Honolulu, Waikiki was the capital of one of Hawaii's great chiefdoms. In the 1400s—around the same time as the European conquest of the Americas—the iconic white-sand bay was made the center of Oahu's government and culture. While its abundant fresh water, ideal for growing taro, was one asset of the location, another was its now-famous surf break. When King Kamehameha I conquered Waikiki in 1795 and united the archipelago's chiefdoms into a unified Hawaiian Kingdom, he moved the capital. But Waikiki remained a favorite vacation and surf spot for Hawaiian nobility, even after the kingdom was annexed by the United States. Hundreds of years later, Waikiki is backed

Waikiki Beach lights up as night falls.

by Honolulu, which retains Hawaiian cultural roots while being among the most cosmopolitan cities in the country.

In South Florida, Miami Beach was a diminutive barrier island topped by a tangle of mangroves until 1915, when savvy investors saw its potential as a tourist destination. Spurred by the recent completion of the Florida East Coast Railway from Jacksonville to Key West, those investors took what was a low-lying strip of sand and salt marsh and radically transformed it, at great expense. Using hired laborers, they filled and dredged, uprooted the mangrove jungle, and built a bridge connecting the island (which

Miami's Ocean Drive runs parallel to the beach and is the epicenter of South Beach's nightlife.

had been artificially increased by 1,200 acres [486 ha], or 75 percent) to the mainland.

In a classic tale of "If we build it, they will come" optimism, Miami Beach went from a picturesque and well-placed sandbar to one of the country's preeminent playgrounds. It's now known as an international party scene, home to the stylish annual Art Basel, an ever-rotating cast of celebrities, and enough trendy beachfront hotels, bars, and restaurants to keep the good times going well after the sun goes down.

A century later, the story was repeated elsewhere. Mexico's tourism authority has a multidecade history of building resort cities from whole cloth. While some of the country's beloved beach destinations started organically, many of the biggest and best known—Cancún, Cabo San Lucas, and Huatulco among them—were planned cities designed to attract foreign investment and tourists. Many of these booming metropoles were little more than fishing villages several decades ago.

In the Middle East, the capital of the United Arab Emirates has even greater ambition and technological savvy. The desert city of Dubai grew from a trading hub of about 10,000 people in 1900 to an oil-boom town in the mid-century to a city of nearly 3.5 million, with the tallest skyscraper in the world and multiple sand-island chains—including Palm Jumeirah and Bluewaters Island—that were not only reimagined, but entirely human-made.

Tropical metropoles where beaches are a year-round focal point may be the first to spring to mind, but there are also northern cities, like Tallinn, Estonia, that are surrounded by beloved beaches. In the summer, Pirita Beach is crowded with everyone from kitesurfers to sunbathers to families barbecuing, while other beaches along the Baltic Sea, like Kakumäe Rand, are quieter, with powdery white sand backed by pine trees.

In other places around the world, the urban beaches—artificial or natural—are more modest. But these beaches are still central to the character of the city, to a sense of carefree fun and an embrace of seasonality and cosmopolitanism. No one would call New York City a "beach town," for example, yet those who know the city well know that its beaches—Coney Island's historic boardwalk,

F

G

the Russian immigrant community of Brighton Beach, the Rockaways' surf scene—are nearly as core to the city's identity as Broadway. Cape Town's Clifton Beaches, Tel Aviv's Gordon Beach, and Singapore's Palawan Beach are all examples of beaches that are central to their cities' cultures, but not their reason for being.

NOTABLE URBAN BEACHES

A CONEY ISLAND BEACH, NEW YORK, U.S.A.: The Wonder Wheel, an attraction since 1920, still draws beachgoers to this coastal New York City amusement park on Jamaica Bay.

B PALM JUMEIRAH, UNITED ARAB EMIRATES: This artificial archipelago on the Persian Gulf is known for high-end hotels, upscale dining, and views of the Dubai coastline.

C PIRITA BEACH, ESTONIA: The largest and most popular beach in Tallinn, Pirita Beach is also well-served by public transit and wheelchair accessible.

D PALAWAN BEACH, SINGAPORE: The southern shore of Sentosa, Singapore, boasts food stalls, bars, and a Skyride offering a bird's-eye view.

E STREETS BEACH, QUEENSLAND, AUSTRALIA: Australia's only inner-city man-made beach is a subtropical oasis for natives and visitors alike in downtown Brisbane.

F CABO SAN LUCAS, MEXICO: Breaching humpback whales are a frequent sight in the waters off the coast of Mexico's premiere playground.

G CLIFTON BEACHES, SOUTH AFRICA: Bonfires, dance festivals, and beachfront dining attract visitors to Cape Town's Clifton Beaches even after the sun goes down.

LAKE McDONALD BEACH

A shoreline carpeted with strikingly colorful stones and backed by mountains

CATEGORY: Unusual   **BEST TIME TO GO: Late June through mid-September**
WHAT YOU'LL EXPERIENCE: Uncommonly clear water, Going-to-the-Sun Road, alpine forests, Lake McDonald

In northern Montana, near the border with Canada, Glacier National Park is a fantasy trip for many mountain wilderness lovers. The park's 50-mile-long (80 km) Going-to-the-Sun Road is often cited among the most breathtaking drives in the world. But the shores of Lake McDonald—Glacier's largest lake—offer an intriguing spin on the park's geological wonders: smooth stones in a spectacular array of seemingly unnatural colors, from reds and purples to greens and yellows. These brilliant hues are made more striking by exceptionally, almost bafflingly clear water.

Lake McDonald is an Ice Age lake that formed by glaciers cutting a 10-mile-long (16 km), nearly 500-foot-deep (152 m) gash through the alpine landscape of hemlock and western red cedar. The lake is just 14 miles (22.5 km) from the Continental Divide and surrounded on three sides by peaks. Fjord-like, the lake's water temperature stays below 50°F (10°C) year-round, creating an environment in which plankton can't grow. This creates water so transparent it has the almost fishbowl-like effect of magnifying everything beneath the surface, making the stones appear even more brilliantly hued.

The mountains around the lake create a relatively humid, temperate climate that attracts some of the park's more spectacular animal species. Black bears, mountain goats, bighorn sheep, and elk are frequent visitors to the valley, making for excellent wildlife viewing.

Bright fall leaves compete with the colored stones that line the bottom of Lake McDonald.

PAPAKŌLEA BEACH

A secluded stretch of prime coastline tinted olive green by volcanic forces

CATEGORY: Unusual   BEST TIME TO GO: April through September
WHAT YOU'LL EXPERIENCE: Eroded cliffs, windswept dunes, crashing waves, Pacific Ocean

There are just four green-sand beaches in the world. Papakōlea Beach, on the south point of the island of Hawaii, is by far the most popular. Its sparkly sand is made up of olivine crystals formed around 49,000 years ago with the eruption of Puʻu Mahana. The cinder cone volcano spewed lava down into the sea. Over millennia, powerful waves eroded the hardened lava, but the relatively heavy element olivine stayed put on the beach.

Getting to this legendary cove is a challenge—and also part of the allure. Visitors come via South Point Road, a two-laner through the Big Island's largely undeveloped and rural southern district, Kaʻū. En route to the parking lot, requisite stops include a farmstand that sells coconut water, freshly baked banana bread, and Spam *musubi* (grilled Spam on rice, wrapped with seaweed), and Ka Lae, the southernmost point of the United States. It was here that historians believe ancient Polynesians first landed on the archipelago.

At Ka Lae, which is west of the beach, you'll likely encounter local fishermen and ill-advised cliff jumpers among the rocks. Be aware: People have died jumping here. It's especially dangerous because the ladder up the cliff is rickety and the current is strong. If you're swept away, the next stop is Antarctica.

The adventure continues from the beach parking lot with a 2.5-mile (4 km) hike through a dusty, windy, hot sand dune. It's exposed to the sun the entire way, so you'll need plenty of water and sun protection. Upon arrival at

OPPOSITE: **A view of Papakōlea Beach from the rim of Puʻu Mahana, a cinder cone that erupted about 49,000 years ago**

PAGES 122-123: **The sand gets its green color from olivine, a common mineral component of lava.**

the beach, you'll be rewarded for your effort with panoramic views over Mahana Bay and the surrounding eroded cliffs that resemble stacks of pancakes. After an exciting scramble down a steep stairway built into the cliff, it's finally time to take photos of your toes in the emerald-hued sand. Swimming is only a good idea if the surf is calm; you're better off seeking out a shady ledge to prepare for the long trek back.

There are locals who make a living shuttling tourists to and from the beach in their trucks. This off-road driving is illegal and destructive to the coastal ecosystems—so opt out. Deep ruts and dirt paths created by the vehicles have harmed sensitive dune plants such as 'ohai, a native shrub with orange and red blossoms. The region is sacred, as the dunes contain *iwi kupuna* (ancient Hawaiian bones) that aren't meant to be disturbed. While it is easier, don't take the ride.

OTHER NOTABLE GREEN-SAND BEACHES AROUND THE WORLD

TALO'FO'FO BEACH, GUAM: When the sun shines brightly, the sand on this popular surf beach glows green thanks to olivine.

PUNTA CORMORANT, ECUADOR: On the Galápagos island of Floreana, olivine has drifted over after volcanic activity nearby and collected on this beach.

LAKE HORNINDALSVATNET, NORWAY: This fjord lake beach turned green thanks to glacial mineral deposits rather than volcanic activity.

POLIHALE BEACH

A secluded, wild, and sacred stretch of sand on the Garden Island's western coast

CATEGORY: Remote   **BEST TIME TO GO:** April through October
WHAT YOU'LL EXPERIENCE: Hawaiian monk seals, Nā Pali Coast cliffs, tide pools, Pacific Ocean

Hawaii's longest stretch of sand is also one of its least accessible. But those willing to make the bumpy journey to Polihale Beach will be rewarded with a 17-mile (27 km) vanilla-sand stunner at the western edge of Kauai.

The beach lies within the 130-acre (52.6 ha) Polihale State Park and is celebrated for its striking views of the towering Nā Pali Coast cliffs, along with vibrant tide pools, breezy beach campsites, and 100-foot-tall (30.5 m) coastal dunes. Native Hawaiians consider this place sacred, as the bones of their ancestors are interred in the dunes and the souls of the dead are said to depart from a nearby, ancient *heiau* (temple) to reach Po, the underworld. The entire beach park was also once a network of villages connected by ancient fishponds.

Rental car companies often prohibit the use of their vehicles on the unpaved access road to Polihale, which winds ominously past a missile facility and an old cemetery on the way to the beach. Although this side of Kauai is known for sunny weather, the occasional rainstorm can also flood the road and make it impassable. Hiking is an option—though it's a strenuous and multiday excursion.

Even on a perfect day, travelers might be deterred by powerful rip currents and no lifeguards, the possibility of encountering tiger sharks, or the $30

OPPOSITE: **The miles-long beach offers stunning views of the high sea cliffs of the Nā Pali Coast.**

PAGES 126-127: **Spinner dolphins are often spotted off Polihale Beach.**

camping permit that must be secured in advance to stay the night. But many of the locals who grew up swimming, fishing, surfing, and camping along this secluded and wild coastline say the same thing: This is the best beach in Hawaii and it's worth all the effort.

From the shore, beachgoers are treated to a view of a seemingly endless ocean out to Ni'ihau, a privately owned island where native Hawaiians live much the same way their ancestors did. Although swimming isn't advisable, the sandy shore is a perfect spot to relax under an umbrella or take a stroll, particularly around sunset when pastel clouds routinely explode across the sky as the sun dips behind the Pacific. When conditions are right, some visitors even witness Hawaii's illustrious "green flash," a brief moment during sunset when a small green disk appears at the top of the sun due to atmospheric refraction.

Although Polihale is usually tranquil, there are times when people drive illegally in the dunes, vandalize areas of the park, and make a ruckus. A new master plan under development by Hawaii's Department of Land and Natural Resources aims to protect the cultural and natural resources within the fragile dune system, including sacred skeletal remains and endangered lau'ehu and 'ohai plants. This is also prime territory for endangered Hawaiian monk seals, which have been known to haul out on the beach and even give birth to pups right on the sand. If you see one, mind your space and give them ample room.

SHIP ISLAND SWIM BEACH

A historically significant barrier island surrounded by beaches

CATEGORY: **Historical**   BEST TIME TO GO: **June through September**
WHAT YOU'LL EXPERIENCE: **Bottlenose dolphins, Fort Massachusetts, seashells, Gulf of Mexico**

Located an hour east of New Orleans and 11 miles (18 km) off the coast of Biloxi, Mississippi, Ship Island is a crescent-shaped barrier island bordered almost entirely by white sand. Now part of the expansive Gulf Islands National Seashore, the spot takes its name from its remarkably deep natural port, which played a key role in U.S. colonial history and earned the island the title of the "Plymouth Rock of the Gulf Coast."

French explorers first took shelter here in 1699, noting that Ship Island provided one of the few protected anchorages between Florida and Texas. In the centuries that followed, the island changed hands between the French, Spanish, and British as colonial powers sought to establish control of the Gulf.

Today, Ship Island is undeveloped except for historic Fort Massachusetts, a boardwalk, and a concession stand with beach gear and snacks. A ferry drops passengers at the island's north end, a half-mile (0.8 km) trek from the swimming beach on the south end. Fans of Ship Island note that while the Gulf Coast near Biloxi has many miles of beach, the water quality closer to the mainland suffers from its placement at the mouth of the Mississippi and the resulting runoff. That makes the barrier islands the best—and some say only—option for ocean swimming in the area. However, there's no shade on the beach, so umbrellas and sunscreen are musts.

HISTORY

During the Civil War, Ship Island became the staging area for Union forces during their successful capture of New Orleans. Up to 18,000 soldiers were based on the island. Among the most famous units were the Second Louisiana Native Guard, one of the first Black regiments in the U.S. Army, who were stationed on Ship Island for three years.

Ship Island's white sand and crystal clear water make it a contender for the prettiest beach in Mississippi.

CANNON BEACH

Ensconced between verdant parks, Cannon Beach is famous for Haystack Rock.

CATEGORY: Iconic   **BEST TIME TO GO:** May through September
WHAT YOU'LL EXPERIENCE: Sea stars, sea anemones, tufted puffins, Pacific Ocean

Just a 90-minute drive from Portland, Oregon, Cannon Beach boasts some of the state's most stunning coastal views and spectacular sunsets. Named after a cannon that washed ashore in the 1800s, the charming beach village is known for its art scene and sits just south of picturesque Ecola State Park, which sprawls across nine miles (14.5 km) of wilderness coastline. Really, though, Cannon Beach is all about the rock—Haystack Rock.

Haystack Rock is a 235-foot-tall (72 m) basalt stack that rises dramatically from the ocean. One of the world's tallest intertidal structures, it served as the backdrop for a famous scene in the '80s cult classic film *The Goonies*. You shouldn't climb Haystack Rock (it's protected within the Oregon Islands National Wildlife Refuge and as a state marine garden), but you can view myriad sea creatures during low tide at its base.

The best time to visit is about an hour before low tide, when the vibrant orange and purple sea stars cling to the rock and bright-green anemones open like underwater flowers. Kids will love learning about the nudibranchs, not just because the word is fun to say, but also because the soft-bodied sea slugs look like they were plucked straight from cartoons.

Look for experts in red jackets from the Haystack Rock Awareness Program (HRAP) to get a rundown on other tide pool critters, including chitons, limpets, and corals. These beach staff members are around between mid-February and

OPPOSITE: Haystack Rock was formed approximately 15 million years ago when basaltic lava flowed down from the old Columbia River Basin.

PAGES 132-133: The most colorful creatures at Cannon Beach are the sea stars visible at low tide.

November during low tides. They often have a few sea creatures available for the public to interact with, but picking up or touching the wildlife is otherwise prohibited. There are also microscopes set up to view the smallest organisms wiggling between the seaweed and barnacles.

Haystack Rock is also home to a bevy of rare birds including the adorable tufted puffin, the unofficial mascot of Cannon Beach. During the winter, the bird's plumage is dark gray. During the summer mating season, however, both males and females undergo a colorful transformation: Their large beaks turn bright orange, the feathers around their face turn white, and cream-colored tufts sprout from their heads.

Local groups host parties when the puffins return for nesting season in the summer. Several other birds compete with the puffins to nest on Haystack Rock, notably the Brandt's cormorant—its throat turns cobalt blue during mating season.

Seals and sea lions are commonly spotted at Cannon Beach, while migrating whales turn up off the coast in winter and spring. A rare cougar sighting near Haystack Rock temporarily closed the beach in 2023—though the chances of that happening again are about as likely as finding the pirate One-Eyed Willy's famous buried treasure. Be sure to check the tide charts before your visit, as you're unlikely to see anything but the rock if you stop by during high tide.

ACADIA NATIONAL PARK, MAINE, U.S.A.

SAND
BEACH

Acadia National Park's only natural beach is composed almost entirely of seashell fragments.

CATEGORY: Nature   **BEST TIME TO GO:** June 15 through September 8, when it is a designated swimming beach
WHAT YOU'LL EXPERIENCE: The Beehive, Great Head, a film set, Gulf of Maine

Four miles (6.4 km) south of Bar Harbor, the aptly named Sand Beach is the only, well, sandy beach in Acadia National Park. It's also a place so cinematically striking that significant scenes from the 1999 movie *The Cider House Rules*, based on a John Irving novel, were filmed here.

A so-called pocket beach (a small beach between headlands), it's tucked away in the Gulf of Maine on Mount Desert Island, protected from the eastern Atlantic swells by the Great Head peninsula and from the south by Old Soaker Island. That positioning allows the beach to accumulate shell material from the abundant waters of Newport Cove without the light, delicate particles being washed away as they are elsewhere along this stretch of rugged coast.

Sand Beach, which is just 300 yards (274 m) wide, is made almost entirely of shell: Some 70 to 80 percent of the beach is composed of calcium carbonate particles (the remains of snails, barnacles, crabs, mussels, and urchins). Despite the cold ocean water here, generally ranging from 50 to 60°F (10 to 15°C)—and posted daily on the parking lot's bulletin board—the beach is popular with swimmers and families.

Flanked by tall cliffs, the beach's vistas include Great Head, the highest cliff on the East Coast, a granite monolith that rises 144 feet (44 m) above the Atlantic. From Sand Beach, you can reach its summit along the Great Head Trail, which offers a dramatic mix of scenery and history.

A bird's-eye view from Beehive Loop of Sand Beach, which is protected by rocky cliffs

Behind the beach, the 450-foot-tall (137 m) "Beehive" rises from a valley. The unusual cliff is among Acadia's most celebrated sights and is what geologists call a roche moutonnée, which is a feature with a steep and jagged mountain on one side and gradually sloping hill on the other. The Beehive can be climbed, though the rung-and-ladder trail is not for amateurs, and it has a lagoon at its base.

OTHER NOTABLE U.S. NATIONAL PARK BEACHES

A CAPE LOOKOUT BEACH, CAPE LOOKOUT NATIONAL SEASHORE, NORTH CAROLINA: Only accessible via a three-mile (5 km) ferry ride from Harkers Island, this beach on the southern reaches of North Carolina's Outer Banks has a historic lighthouse, a herd of wild horses, and primitive camping.

B PADRE ISLAND NATIONAL SEASHORE, TEXAS: In notable contrast to its party-happy neighbor, South Padre Island, the northern 66-mile (106 km) portion of this wild coastline is the longest stretch of undeveloped barrier island in the world.

C CANAVERAL NATIONAL SEASHORE, FLORIDA: This barrier island on Florida's Space Coast, south of Daytona, has 24 miles (39 km) of undeveloped beach that offers the occasional manatee sighting. Another sighting you might witness: spaceship launches from nearby Kennedy Space Center and Cape Canaveral Space Force Station.

D TRUNK BAY BEACH, VIRGIN ISLANDS NATIONAL PARK, U.S. VIRGIN ISLANDS: Comprising some 7,000 acres (2,833 ha) of St. John, the least developed of the three keys in the Virgin Islands chain, this Caribbean park protects marine habitat, including seagrass beds and coral reefs (check out the Underwater Snorkel Trail), as well as tropical forests and white-sand coral beaches. The horseshoe-shaped Trunk Bay is especially photogenic.

E POINT DUME STATE PRESERVE, SANTA MONICA MOUNTAINS NATIONAL RECREATION AREA, CALIFORNIA: At legendary Point Dume State Beach, at the base of a tall bluff and a long wooden staircase in Malibu, you can do everything from tide pooling to surfing to watching newborn gray whale calves during their migration (December through March) in the world's largest urban national park.

F BARTLETT COVE BEACH, GLACIER BAY NATIONAL PARK AND PRESERVE, ALASKA: This rocky beach backed by spruce and hemlock trees in the otherwise wild and untamed Glacier Bay has a public boat dock, the historic Glacier Bay Lodge, and a walk-in campground with a firepit on the beach.

PART TWO

SOUTH AMERICA & ANTARCTICA

The Morro Dois Irmãos overlooks iconic Ipanema Beach in Brazil, a draw for surfers and everyone else who visits Rio de Janeiro (page 168).

ANAKENA BEACH

Enigmatic statues from an ancient civilization stand guard on this far-flung beach.

CATEGORY: Historical   **BEST TIME TO GO:** December through March
WHAT YOU'LL EXPERIENCE: White coral sand, Rapa Nui culture, wild horses, Pacific Ocean

Some 2,200 miles (3,540 km) off the western coast of Chile, the coral white sand of Rapa Nui's Anakena Beach is a departure from an otherwise rugged, volcanic landscape. According to legend, this beach was where the first settlers, the Rapa Nui people, came ashore, having traveled more than a thousand miles (1,600 km) across the Pacific from Polynesia in double-hulled sailing canoes. Anakena is also the location of seven *moai*—mysterious, giant statues carved centuries ago by the island's original inhabitants to embody the deified spirits of ancestral chiefs.

Easter Island's coastline is mostly jagged and fringed by jet-black basalt, meaning beaches are rare. The main exception, Anakena Beach on the north side of the island, is defined by clusters of palm trees, white sand, and indigo water, which together create an inarguably tranquil retreat that's long been popular with both tourists and locals. It doesn't hurt that wild horses frequent the area and wildflowers explode with color from time to time. The scenic beachfront also offers amenities for visitors, including two small restaurants, some souvenir stands, and a campground (call ahead to be sure it's open).

The most alluring feature of Anakena Beach, though, is the set of seven moai atop a ceremonial platform, known locally as Ahu Nau Nau, a short walk from the shore. These enigmatic, towering figures highlight the ingenuity of the island's Indigenous inhabitants—we still don't know exactly how they

Dancers perform near Ahu Tahai, the largest and best-restored archaeological site on Rapa Nui.

were made or transported, and research is ongoing. Across Rapa Nui, there are more than 1,000 moai, standing 13 feet (4 m) tall and weighing 11 to 13 tons (10 to 12 mt), on average. Many are complete with both heads and torsos; some are partially or completely buried. Researchers have theorized that the statues provided a way of communicating with deceased ancestors and chiefs, whose supernatural powers could be harnessed for the benefit of humanity. Note that touching the moai is illegal, as they are considered sacred.

A little more than 40 percent of Rapa Nui is designated as Rapa Nui National Park, a UNESCO World Heritage site established to preserve the island's natural and cultural treasures. When you're finished relaxing on the beach, explore archaeological sites such as the moai quarry of Rano Raraku and the ceremonial village of Orongo, trek along scenic trails, or spend time learning about Rapa Nui traditions.

One scenic trail worth meandering is the North Coast Walk, which stretches more than 12 miles (19 km) from Anakena Beach to the island's tallest volcano, Terevaka, and winds past a ceremonial complex, several ancient cave dwellings, and cliff-top rocks with petroglyphs. Just a few minutes east of Anakena is Ovahe Beach, a less-visited shoreline that's good for swimming, along with plenty more volcanic terrain to explore, and a quarry where most of the island's moai were made.

The snorkeling at Anakena is also quite impressive, with rocky areas along the sides of the bay offering opportunities to spot surgeonfish, blue-striped orange tamarins, and the endemic Easter Island butterfly fish. If the surf is rough, don't get close to the rocks, as a strong wave could toss you against them.

Although it's kind of a schlep to get to Rapa Nui (its airport, Mataveri International, is known as the most remote in the world), the time to go is now. In 2022, a fire caused damage to some of the moai, which now have cracks in their interiors. More frequent heavy rains may cause the statues to crumble, and rising seas due to climate change are also a pressing threat.

Moai lined up under the Milky Way on Rapa Nui (Easter Island)

ABOVE: Finished and unfinished moai dot the slopes of Rano Raraku volcano in Rapa Nui National Park—the quarry for all the giant statues.

OPPOSITE: Anakena Beach is one of the few white-sand beaches on Rapa Nui.

WHAT IS CORAL SAND?

Many white-sand beaches are composed mostly of quartz—but not all. Sometimes a beach is made of coral sand. This type of sand contains not only fragments of actual coral, but also remnants of tiny marine animals, algae, mollusks, and crustaceans. The fragments are made of calcium carbonate (the same stuff that makes up coral skeletons and shells) that have been broken down over time by waves and various sea creatures. If you hear anyone say that parrotfish poop becomes sand at the beach, well, this is the sort of beach they're talking about.

SAINT ANDREWS BAY

A remote beach where king penguins gather by the hundreds of thousands

CATEGORY: **Wildlife**   BEST TIME TO GO: **November through January**
WHAT YOU'LL EXPERIENCE: **Glaciers, elephant seals, reindeer, Atlantic Ocean**

Imagine a wide beach where the shore is crowded not with sun loungers and tanning bodies but with a colony of some 150,000 pairs of king penguins. That's what you'll find on the beach of this Antarctic bay—host to the largest such penguin colony in the world. With their distinctive black-and-white bodies and a splash of bright orange on their ears and chest, individuals from the second-largest penguin species are striking on their own, but a true spectacle when gathered by the tens of thousands.

Near the hamlet of Grytviken, the beach at St. Andrews Bay is just south of Mount Skittle, the 1,575-foot-tall (480 m) mountain that's a South Georgia landmark, surrounded by four snowy peaks, grassy plains, and receding glaciers. The island was first explored in 1775 by British explorer Captain James Cook. Today, it is a wildlife photographer's dream: In addition to the king penguin colony, there's also a large population of elephant seals and reindeer that cling to the slopes nearby.

Until the 1970s, Cook Glacier abutted St. Andrews Bay. In the years since, it has retreated significantly, as have most of the glaciers on the island over the past 60 years. The gravel beach and bay are remnants of an Antarctic landscape that is being transformed by climate change. Because of the remoteness and harsh environment here, South Georgia is generally only accessible to visitors through an experienced tour company.

King penguins parade past elephant seals on the beach of St. Andrews Bay.

PLAYA ROJA

Stunning wind- and water-carved cliffs frame this red-sand beach.

CATEGORY: Wildlife   BEST TIME TO GO: December through March, April through November for penguins
WHAT YOU'LL EXPERIENCE: Paracas Candelabra prehistoric geoglyph, Humboldt penguins, Pacific Ocean

Paracas National Reserve's captivatingly barren landscape of orange desert plains, cliffs, and dunes is one of Peru's most dramatic sights. The expansive park, near the town of Pisco—famous for its eponymous beverage—has magnificent sea- and wind-carved cliffs made from pink granodiorite, a form of volcanic solidified magma. Between Playa Lagunillas and Punta Santa Maria, the coast has eroded to form a rust-red beach, aptly named Playa Roja, set against these ocher cliffs. The vistas from the lookout provide an otherworldly sight few beaches can match.

Paracas National Reserve, a UNESCO-protected area since 1975, is best known for Candelabra, an ancient carving resembling a candlestick etched into a hillside. The geoglyph is 600 feet (180 m) high and dates to the Paracas culture, from approximately 800 B.C. to 100 B.C., which predates the Nasca. Like with the better-known nearby Nasca Lines, the image is large enough to be seen from far away—some say as far as 12 miles (19 km) out at sea.

The park is also a jumping-off point for the Ballestas Islands, which are sometimes referred to as the poor man's Galápagos. The uninhabited islands—many covered in guano, once one of Peru's major exports—are home to Humboldt penguins, guanay cormorants, fur seals, and blue-footed boobies.

Swimming is not allowed at Playa Roja, but it is possible at other beaches in the park, including Playa La Mina and Playa El Raspón.

The red sand of Playa Roja is the result of the erosion of ancient lava.

CABO SAN JUAN DEL GUÍA

A popular swimming spot near a famous jungle hike to a pre-Columbian settlement

CATEGORY: Historical   **BEST TIME TO GO:** September through November
WHAT YOU'LL EXPERIENCE: Sierra Nevada de Santa Marta, palm-fringed coves, Caribbean Sea

On Colombia's wild Caribbean coastline, the dripping rainforest and the Sierra Nevada de Santa Marta mountain range meet the sea in Tayrona National Park. The park encompasses 58 square miles (150 km²) of land and 12 square miles (30 km²) of protected sea. The prettiest and most popular beach is Cabo San Juan del Guía, which features a pair of back-to-back coves and a spit of land leading to a small, rocky hill at the center. On top of that hill is a gazebo filled with hammocks. You have not experienced true relaxation until you've nestled into one of those hammocks while gazing out over the blue-green Caribbean.

Unlike most of the other beaches up and down this coastline, where the ocean is typically treacherous, Cabo San Juan del Guía is a protected cove and a great place to swim. There's also a restaurant right on the beach serving up fresh seafood and fruit juices, along with several options for overnight stays, including tents, cabins, and hammocks if you want to sleep under the stars. It's optimal to make this your home base while you spend multiple days exploring the vast park, a remarkably biodiverse UNESCO Biosphere Reserve and the home of the Kogi people, one of several Indigenous groups that descended from the area's original inhabitants, the Tairona.

The most adventurous travelers gravitate toward the park's keystone attraction: a four-day guided hike to Ciudad Perdida (Lost City), a Kogi

OPPOSITE: Cabo San Juan del Guía is one of the most popular beaches in Tayrona National Park.

PAGES 152-153: Beachgoers often wade out to the rocks off the beach at Cabo San Juan del Guía.

settlement high in the mountains that was abandoned before the Spanish invaded. The majority of visitors stop by the park on day trips, however, and usually make Cabo San Juan del Guía their prime destination. Many arrive in speedboats from Bahía de Taganga near Santa Marta, a 30-minute journey. Others make the drive to the El Zaino entrance, which takes about an hour from Taganga.

Keep in mind, from the early 1970s until the early 2000s, the park was controlled by paramilitary groups and wasn't particularly safe. Armed groups and coca growers still operate in some of the more remote regions of the park. Plan to stay on the beaten path and keep your eyes peeled. Aside from any suspicious human behavior, you may also spot monkeys in the treetops and the occasional jaguar roaming the sandy shoreline.

NEARBY BEACHES

BOCA DEL SACO: A short walk from Cabo San Juan del Guía through a scrubby forest, this beach tends to attract nude sunbathers. It is rarely crowded, but swimming is a bad idea.

ARRECIFES: A big sandy beach backed by jungle-covered mountains, it's between the park entrance and Cabo San Juan. There are campsites and a few small restaurants. The sunsets are sensational. Don't swim.

LA PISCINA: A beach where you can swim! Along this stretch of calm, tranquil coves, rocks form a pool, and the whole area is protected by an offshore reef. Snorkelers love to plunge in here and gawk at the tropical fish.

BALNEARIO EL CÓNDOR

At the edge of Patagonia, a beach where burrowing parrots own the cliffs

CATEGORY: Wildlife   **BEST TIME TO GO:** December through January is parrot breeding season
WHAT YOU'LL EXPERIENCE: Sandstone cliffs, wind sports, fishing, Río Negro

The mighty Río Negro flows all the way from the Andes to the Atlantic, an epic route through the vast steppes of Argentine Patagonia. The province that shares its name nestles in the southern cone of South America. The area's standout beach, Balneario El Cóndor, is better known among locals as La Boca, a reference to its location at the mouth of the river, where the water tends toward a more earthy hue than a true blue.

This is just south of Argentina's breadbasket, a series of fertile valleys that spill into the Atlantic, some 18 miles (30 km) from the provincial capital, Viedma. A long coastline of wide beach—formally named for the *Condor*, a Danish ship that was wrecked here in 1881—is a major draw for visitors during the Southern Hemisphere's summer. From December through February, La Boca is crowded with sunbathers, wind sports enthusiasts, and shore fishers. It can get hot during the high season: Temperatures sometimes reach into the low 100s Fahrenheit (38°C), though the high 70s Fahrenheit (24°C) are more common. Water temperatures are typically a bit chilly for swimming, but pleasantly refreshing during the hottest, driest Patagonian days.

La Boca is best known as the home of the largest colony of burrowing parrots, or Patagonian conures, in the world, with an average of 37,000 burrowing parrot nests. The beach is backed by towering sandstone cliffs that are clustered with a fluttering spectacle of small, olive-colored birds.

PROTECTING WILDLIFE

Burrowing parrots are threatened due to climate change and habitat loss. They spend months of each year digging deep into the walls of the cliffs, where they lay their eggs directly on a bed of sand. They return season after season, deepening their burrows each year. Scientists are advocating for further protections and urge visitors to park at least a mile away and walk.

Two members of the world's largest colony of burrowing parrots take flight.

UNESCO BEACHES

The organization's World Heritage sites include many with stunning shorelines.

World Heritage sites are selected by the United Nations Educational, Scientific and Cultural Organization (UNESCO) for their outstanding universal value, and to merit this distinction, a site must meet strict criteria. The sites can qualify on either natural or cultural grounds, and after undergoing extensive evaluations by experts, they are nominated by their host countries. In the end, only the most exceptional places—those with irreplaceable value to humanity—earn this recognition.

Places as unique and diverse as the wilds of East Africa's Serengeti, Machu Picchu in Peru, the striped Danxia landform in China, and Iguazú Falls in Argentina are among the more than 1,200 sites found across 168 countries. Beyond the areas profiled in this book—which include Bonaire National Marine Park (page 29), the Gulf of California (page 72), Fernando de Noronha (page 162), and Rapa Nui National Park (page 143)—here is a handful with stunning beaches.

LAGOONS OF NEW CALEDONIA, FRANCE: Designated a World Heritage site in 2008 for its natural beauty and exceptional diversity, this site of six marine clusters in the South Pacific features teeming coral reefs that support a vast array of life, including turtles, whales, and dugongs. The surrounding white-sand beaches are ideal launch points to explore this underwater sanctuary.

The sun sets over the soft sand beaches of New Caledonia.

A PORTOVENERE, CINQUE TERRE, AND THE ISLANDS, ITALY: These seaside Italian enclaves received their World Heritage site designation in 1997, earning the recognition for extraordinary value as a cultural landscape. Between the five cliffside fishing villages of Cinque Terre, you'll find craggy coves and sublime stretches of sand.

B STONE TOWN OF ZANZIBAR, TANZANIA: On a promontory overlooking the Indian Ocean, this seaside Swahili trading town has been a hub of African, Indian, European, and Middle Eastern culture for a thousand years. The town's wooden carved doors, bustling street bazaars, and enchanting seafront mansions are just a short distance from Zanzibar's loveliest shorelines.

C REDWOOD NATIONAL AND STATE PARKS, CALIFORNIA, U.S.A.: The spectacular parks are where the crashing Pacific meets California's coastal mountains, and they are home to the world's tallest and most awe-inspiring trees. Myriad forest hikes end in golden sand beaches, with spectacular views of the jagged shoreline and nearby rock stacks and islets.

D TUBBATAHA REEFS NATURAL PARK, PHILIPPINES: At the center of the Sulu Sea, this unique park features a thriving atoll reef that supports an abundance of marine life, including nearly 700 species of fish, along with nesting seabirds and marine turtles. Visitors frequent the park's two coral islands en route to exploring the expansive lagoons.

E K'GARI, QUEENSLAND, AUSTRALIA: The world's largest sand island lies off the east coast of Australia. The island is home to tropical rainforests, shifting sand dunes, endless white-sand beaches, and freshwater lakes, which are better for swimming due to the strong surf and currents in the oceans.

PRAIA DA ILHA DO AMOR

A river beach at a colonial Portuguese outpost deep in the Brazilian Amazon

CATEGORY: Lake, river, and waterway   **BEST TIME TO GO:** August through December
WHAT YOU'LL EXPERIENCE: Festa do Sairé, Borari Indigenous culture, Tapajós River

nto the 18th century, Alter do Chão—a village deep in the Brazilian Amazon where sloths and howler monkeys hang in the jungle overhead—was inhabited largely by the Indigenous Borari people. But as Jesuit missionaries made their way to the area, the Portuguese established themselves on the sandy banks of the Tapajós River. Soon, this landlocked beach town developed a romantic, almost mystical reputation.

Alter do Chão's location on an ancient sand dune between the river and Lago Verde has made it an economic and cultural crossroads, as well as a geographic novelty: a white-sand beach far from the sea.

That unusual geography has also made Alter do Chão, and the community that lives there, vulnerable to rising water and shifting sand. Depending on the Amazon River's flow, the beach, called Praia da Ilha do Amor (Love Island Beach), may only be accessible six months a year, and submerged the rest. But efforts are being made to save this rare Amazonian beach, where the river water is warm and clear enough to snorkel, and *barracas*—casual, thatched-roof beach restaurants—serve the local beer, Tijuca, to bohemian beachgoers.

Alter do Chão is reachable by boat, including a flotilla of canoes that ferry visitors to its shores for a modest price. Popular day trips include river boat tours to the Canal do Jari to see piranha-filled lakes, tucuxis and pink dolphins, and giant water lily pads that can reach 10 feet (3 m) in diameter.

FESTIVAL

The village's 300-year-old Festa do Sairé, which mixes Portuguese and Indigenous cultural traditions in a four-day celebration, can draw up to 100,000 visitors.

A bird's-eye view of the landlocked beach town of Alter do Chão

FERNANDO DE NORONHA, BRAZIL

BAÍA DO SANCHO

A hard-to-reach, stunning shoreline beneath soaring cliffs on a remote archipelago

CATEGORY: Remote   **BEST TIME TO GO:** December through March
WHAT YOU'LL EXPERIENCE: Soft white sand, blue-green water, Atlantic Ocean

Some 326 miles (525 km) off the coast of Brazil, the volcanic archipelago Fernando de Noronha is replete with lovely beaches. But Baía do Sancho is the loveliest of all. Many visitors rank Sancho as the best beach in the world, and for years it held that top distinction on Tripadvisor. That's probably thanks to its beauty—and remoteness. The crescent of soft white sand lies at the foot of tall, craggy cliffs cloaked in dense groves of fruit and nut trees and medicinal shrubs. Sea turtles and dolphins frequent these waters, along with seabirds that regularly visit the cliffs. But few people find their way to this tropical sanctuary, which is part of Brazil's first national marine park and a UNESCO World Heritage site.

To reach Baía do Sancho, visitors must fly from mainland Brazil, departing from either Recife or Natal, to the main island of Fernando de Noronha. Before visiting Sancho, accessed via a short drive west of the airport, visitors must pay an environmental tax and a park entry fee (around $70 total) at the beach's park office. This can be done in advance online (which saves time), or in person on the island. The steep price goes to the good cause of supporting the marine park. The pass is good for 10 days and allows access to all hiking trails and beaches around the island, which is more than worth it.

Once all the logistics are taken care of, head through the gift shop to a walkway and through some greenery on your way to the beach. After about

The cliffs that surround Baía do Sancho offer a spectacular view.

> *"When you're in the water, it's a moment that you forget everything else."*
>
> —ÍTALO FERREIRA, BRAZILIAN SURFER

10 minutes (which can be extremely hot, depending on the time of year), you'll come to an observation deck that overlooks the beach about 100 feet (30 m) below. There, an employee will tell you when to begin your descent on a vertical ladder. The first ladder is rickety, cuts through a rock wall, and ends at a narrow tunnel, which leads to a second, even more rickety ladder. (Keep an eye out for large iguanas around these parts.) Finally, a few uneven, sandy steps lead down to the beach.

If that journey sounds uncomfortable, you can also visit Baía do Sancho on a morning boat tour. Although this way offers the chance to scuba dive in crystal clear water with sea turtles and rays, it also means you won't be on the beach during the best time for suntanning (the afternoon). Regardless of when you come, snorkeling is a fantastic idea. At either end of the beach there are pools chiseled into the lava rock that are usually full of colorful fish. Turtles spawn here between January and July, so be aware the beach is closed between 6 p.m. and 6 a.m. during those months.

One of the best things about Baía do Sancho is that you're likely to have it mostly to yourself. The infrastructure on the Fernando de Noronha archipelago only supports a few hundred tourists and a few thousand locals. With 17 gorgeous beaches across the chain, Baía do Sancho is one of the more challenging beaches to access—leaving space for braver souls.

Beyond the beaches, there's a ton of interesting history across the archipelago. The area was once a penal colony and a missile tracking station for the United States during the Cold War. It was only in 1988 that the national marine park was born, but the results are undeniably spectacular.

Abundant marine life can be found in the crystal clear water.

A

B

C

D

NEARBY BEACHES

A BAÍA DOS PORCOS: Small but mighty, Baía dos Porcos is a golden sand beach dotted with volcanic rocks and lapped by gentle blue-green waves. Views of the nearby Morro Dois Irmãos (a pair of volcanic islets protruding from the sea) are spectacular. Be sure to go at low tide, as access is only via a headland from neighboring Praia Cacimba do Padre.

B PRAIA DO LEÃO: If it's isolation you seek, this rugged and wild shoreline is for you. The long, tawny beach gives way to clear blue water and interesting rock formations, and there's rarely another soul here.

C PRAIA DO SUESTE: Located on the south coast, Praia do Sueste is the easiest beach to reach and is a great place to snorkel and spot turtles and baby sharks.

D PRAIA DA CACIMBA DO PADRE: This long expanse of fluffy vanilla sand and clear turquoise water also offers a stellar view of the iconic Morro Dois Irmãos. Walk along the mossy hills to the west for a good look at the beach from above.

IPANEMA BEACH

The trendsetting beach that brought bossa nova and Brazilian beach culture to the world

---

CATEGORY: Iconic   **BEST TIME TO GO:** Year-round; December through March is peak season
WHAT YOU'LL EXPERIENCE: Surfing at Pedra do Arpoador, *futevôlei* and *frescobol*, Atlantic Ocean

Known worldwide for its distinctive waterfront promenade and its pride of place in the swaying bossa nova song "The Girl from Ipanema," Ipanema Beach—and the stylish neighborhood that surrounds it—seems to stay with everyone who comes under its spell. It's a feast for the senses: the smell of skewered oregano-seasoned *coalho* cheese, grilled on a stick; the subcultures that congregate around the numbered *postos* (lifeguard towers) along the beach; the skyline-defining Dois Irmãos (Two Brothers) mountains.

This stretch of Rio de Janeiro's shore is typically a bit more relaxed—less crowded and frenetic—than its conjoined twin, Copacabana. Like any urban beach worth its salt, 1.5-mile-long (2.4 km) Ipanema is a place where different kinds of people share a patch of sand and sea, their varying interests overlapping to create a distinct beach culture.

Here, that means games of *futevôlei* (a Brazilian version of volleyball played without hands) and *frescobol* (a tennis-like game without a net played with wooden paddles). It means surfers in the waves, where winter brings nine-foot (3 m) swells that vary from a surfable barrel to a dangerous shore break. It means beautiful jet-setters rubbing shoulders with grungy backpackers. But what it really means is a cultural experience in one of the most romantic spots in the world.

WHAT'S IN A NAME?

Somewhat ironically, considering the beach's romantic reputation, its name means "bad, dangerous waters" in the Indigenous Tupi language.

Beachgoers play *futevôlei* as the sun sets over Ipanema.

PLAYA RÁBIDA

Explore volcanic red sand frequented by seabirds, sea lions, and marine iguanas.

CATEGORY: **Nature**   BEST TIME TO GO: **December through May**
WHAT YOU'LL EXPERIENCE: **Flamingos, booby birds, nesting pelicans, Pacific Ocean**

Welcome to Mars! Okay, Rábida Island's beach is not actually Mars, but its deep red-hued sand and steep, cinder slopes certainly pass for alien territory. Add to the equation that there are no humans living on this small island off the coast of the larger Santiago Island, and yes, you may think you've landed on the red planet. You're here for the wildlife, though, which is abundant and not at all extraterrestrial.

Visitors regularly arrive on Rábida via a wet landing on the beach, which is exactly what it sounds like: You wade a short distance from a moored boat to the island's northern shore. On arrival, the first thing most people notice is the nearly blood-colored sand, an effect of the high iron content in the lava that formed the island. Noisy sea lions and unassuming marine iguanas may also grab your attention along the rocky coastline, but a short hike inland leads to a salty lagoon where flamingos occasionally stop by to feed on their favorite snack: pink shrimp larva. Note the "occasionally"—there are some years the flamingos simply don't show up.

Other bird sightings are more predictable: Brown pelicans nest in the salt brush behind the beach, and blue-footed and Nazca boobies can be seen in the cliffs above. Nine kinds of finches—the avian species that helped Darwin make these remarkable islands so famous—as well as yellow warblers,

OPPOSITE: **Rábida Beach is home to a large and noisy colony of sea lions.**

PAGES 172-173: **The red sand of Rábida is due to the high iron content in the lava that formed the island.**

mockingbirds, and Galápagos doves can also be spotted among the island's cacti, palo santo trees, and scrubby bushes.

An obvious, solitary path up the cliff takes about 20 minutes to complete, and culminates with a fabulous view of both the lagoon and the coastline. Plunging into the water at the rocky east end of the beach for snorkeling or scuba diving also has rewards: schools of reef fish, cruising sea turtles, and an array of rays and sharks.

NEARBY BEACHES

TORTUGA BAY: A 30-minute walk from Puerto Ayora on Santa Cruz Island, this is the most popular beach in the Galápagos Islands. Marine iguanas often laze around in the sand before plunging into the turquoise water to hunt algae. Turtle nesting season stretches from January through March, and eggs hatch after a two-month incubation.

PLAYA DORADA (GOLDEN BEACH): This crescent-shaped cove is beloved for its location at the base of the iconically spiky Pinnacle Rock on Bartolomé Island, just east of Santiago Island. Cruise ship passengers regularly visit, as do sea turtles, Galápagos penguins, and sea lions. Snorkeling is a great idea here.

GARDNER BAY: Tucked away on remote Española Island, this coral white-sand dream is most often visited by cruise ship passengers, as it's a 10- to 12-hour boat ride from Santa Cruz Island. A sea lion colony plies the waters, while albatrosses and blue-footed boobies soar above.

BEACH EATS

Sweets, salty treats, and seafood are perfect complements to a day at the shore.

Nearly every country that has a shoreline has some kind of beach snack—from regional seafood dishes, to sweet treats, to icy desserts, to almost anything on a stick. Perhaps due to the limitations of preparing and serving food on the beach, or to the festive mood that accompanies a trip to the seaside, beach food is often as novel as it is refreshing.

Anywhere there are fishers, there's likely a seafood-centric beach specialty. Bahamian conch fritters, Spanish *boquerones fritos* (fried anchovies), Peruvian ceviche (raw citrus-marinated fish), and southern Thai fish curries are just a few.

Though a relatively new addition to the canon of popular seaside fare, the New England lobster roll is now a global delicacy. Said to have originated at a restaurant called Perry's in Milford, Connecticut, in the late 1920s, the roll has proliferated up and down the New England coastline—and around the world—in the past 100 years. There is now an entire restaurant chain, Homer Lobster, devoted to lobster rolls, with multiple locations in Paris, as well as outposts in Saint-Tropez and Dubai. In Taiwan, McDonald's launched a limited-run lobster roll in 2023 that quickly became a cult menu item.

Sweet treats go well with sand and salt air. Think of the Croatian *krofne* (filled donuts) sold by wandering beach vendors, or saltwater taffy on New Jersey boardwalks.

Lobster roll, which originated on the coast of New England

Hawaiian shave (not shaved) ice is a category all its own. It crossed the Pacific Ocean from Japan—where it's known as *kakigōri*—to the United States, the Philippines, Latin America, and beyond. In each country and region, the preparation is distinctive, with variations that embrace different shapes and types of ice (crushed or fluffy, heaped or shaped into a ball) and all types of flavors, syrups, toppings, and accompaniments.

Filipino *halo-halo*, for example, likely came to the Philippines with Japanese immigrant workers in the early 20th century. It couldn't have existed, however, without the equally significant arrival of ice from the United States, first in the form of blocks shipped from Massachusetts in the late 1800s, then from a U.S.-owned ice factory in Manila. In the Philippines, shaved ice became one of the country's most notable national dishes, with a range of toppings as sprawling as the Philippine archipelago's 7,641 islands—everything from *ube* ice cream, sweetened kidney beans, boiled taro, agar-agar, and fruit preserves top the chilly treat. A showy cousin to Japan's traditional kakigōri, halo-halo is a complex and brightly colored concoction, with layers of flavor and texture.

Hawaiian shave ice shares traits of its Japanese forebears, with fluffy ice and tropical fruit syrups, while its U.S. mainland cousin, the snow cone, is a boardwalk favorite with a crunchier, pellet-like texture and primary-colored artificial flavors evoking mid-century culinary novelty.

When it comes to skewered foods, the advantages are obvious: They can be cooked over an open fire or in a mobile fry cart and are easy to eat without dishes or utensils. There's an entire genre of food on a stick that goes beyond corn on the cob (which is sold by vendors from Thailand to Mexico), and includes everything from Korean skewered fish cakes to grilled cheese (Brazilian *queijo coalho*), squid (*ang dtray-meuk* in Cambodia), and shrimp on the beaches of Mexico's Pacific coast. And don't forget the mid-century U.S. classics like corn dogs and cotton candy.

Iconic beach eats can be many things, but there are through lines across cultures. This is food fresh from the sea, or food that's casual, celebratory, refreshing, and easy to eat while sitting on the sand, skin salty from seawater.

A: Brightly colored halo-halo from the Philippines

B: Floating food market in Krabi, Thailand

C: Crispy fried anchovies are a seaside favorite in Spain and along the Black Sea.

D: Saltwater taffy originated in Atlantic City, New Jersey.

E: Grilled squid on a stick is popular in Cambodia and other Asian countries.

In hotter climates, it might be spicy, like Jamaican jerk chicken or Mumbai's *pani puri*—a deep-fried shell of dough stuffed with a range of spiced fillings and a cold soup of spicy, fragrant "water." Cooler climates might favor heartier dishes, like New England's clam chowder, which traveled west to Northern California, where it's served in a sourdough bread bowl.

Sometimes it's a beloved establishment that makes a beach food iconic. Take, for example, the Nathan's hot dog—a Coney Island institution since 1916, when Nathan's was started in New York's quintessential beach community by Polish immigrant Nathan Handwerker. Joe's Stone Crab Restaurant and Take Away in Miami Beach is even older, opening in 1913, when Miami Beach was not yet a city. In Southern California's San Diego, Rubio's Coastal Grill opened in 1983, and in just four decades made the fish taco a coastal California staple. Rubio's, now a chain with more than 80 locations, may not make the best or most authentic beer-battered fried fish tacos, but its success shows how a single trip to the beach—in this case Ralph Rubio's surf trip to San Felipe, Baja—can transform local food culture.

A: Baja California-style fish and shrimp tacos

B: Toppings for shave ice vary by country.

C: Red tuna and whitefish ceviche is a traditional dish of Peru.

PLAYA BRAVA

In a city of beaches, Playa Brava stands out for its iconic sculpture.

CATEGORY: **Culture**   BEST TIME TO GO: **October through March**
WHAT YOU'LL EXPERIENCE: **La Mano de Punta del Este, food stands, nightlife, Atlantic Ocean**

Not long ago, Punta del Este was a small town. With a population of about 15,000, it still barely qualifies as a city. But this "Monaco of the South" has an urban skyline of condo towers and a seasonal influx that makes it seem large. The lure of this jet-set beach town—where Argentines, Brazilians, and Europeans flock—is the city's unusually long 20-mile (32 km) coastline and magnificent, varied beaches. Most iconic among them is the Atlantic-facing Playa Brava, also known as Playa de los Dedos (Beach of the Fingers) for its famous La Mano (The Hand) sculpture.

The imposing piece of public art, made in 1982, is the work of Chilean artist Mario Irarrázabal. Constructed over six days as part of the International Meeting of Modern Sculpture in the Open Air, the piece looks like a hand partially submerged in the sand, fingers reaching to the sky. It has become a landmark and helped put Playa Brava on the map.

The long, wide beach of clean, golden sand has rough water (*brava* can mean "rough" in Spanish) and is better for surfing and sunbathing than swimming, although there are lifeguards on duty for those who want to experience the cool, clear water.

Those looking for calmer waters can travel to the west side of the peninsula to visit the aptly named Playa Mansa (*mansa* means "calm" in Spanish), which faces the Río de la Plata.

OPPOSITE: **The sun rises over Playa Brava's La Mano, a sculpture by Chilean artist Mario Irarrázabal.**

PAGES 182-183: **The waves can be rough off the beach at Playa Brava.**

BEACH SCULPTURES AROUND THE WORLD

SERPENT D'OCÉAN, SAINT-BREVIN-LES-PINS, FRANCE: Installed in the intertidal zone, this 2012 work by artist Huang Yong Ping depicts the skeleton of a sea serpent. The 426-foot-long (130 m) aluminum sculpture was built as part of the "Estuaire" art exhibition.

KING NEPTUNE STATUE, VIRGINIA BEACH, VIRGINIA, U.S.A.: Created in 2005, this 34-foot-tall (10 m) cast bronze sculpture of Neptune by artist Paul DiPasquale reflects the sun and depicts the sea god with a trident in one hand and the other hand resting on a loggerhead turtle.

INUKSHUK MONUMENT, ENGLISH BAY, VANCOUVER, BRITISH COLUMBIA, CANADA: Used as place markers by the Inuit of northern Canada, Inukshuk ("in the likeness of a human") are traditionally built from whatever rocks are on-site and constructed so that the limbs indicate directions for navigation. The piece was commissioned by the Northwest Territories for the EXPO 86 world's fair in Vancouver and was later given to the city, which placed it on the east side of Vancouver's English Bay Beach.

PEIX (FISH), BARCELONETA BEACH, BARCELONA, SPAIN: Frank Gehry's 184-foot-long (56 m) and 115-foot-high (35 m) metal fish sculpture, built for the 1992 Summer Olympics, is visible from Barceloneta Beach. The landmark statue looks as if it's about to leap into the Mediterranean.

TE PUKA (THE ANCHOR STONE), STEWART ISLAND (RAKIURA), NEW ZEALAND: A massive metal anchor chain crossing a popular path on Stewart Island (Rakiura), this striking piece of public art represents the Māori legend that the larger South Island of New Zealand was the canoe of demigod Māui and the smaller Stewart Island was the boat's anchor stone.

SAUNDERS ISLAND

A remote and rugged South Atlantic island doubling as a coastal wildlife destination

CATEGORY: **Wildlife**   BEST TIME TO GO: **September through April**
WHAT YOU'LL EXPERIENCE: **Penguins, albatrosses, sheep, Atlantic Ocean**

Hidden away in a far-flung corner of the South Atlantic within the Falkland Islands, Saunders Island is home to thousands of penguins and sheep, but the number of humans can be tallied on one hand. Although the British settled the island briefly in 1765, it's been in the hands of the Pole-Evans family since 1987. The family runs a sheep farm on the island and has also made it a tourist destination.

Visitors tend to enjoy the hiking, as well as the sweeping vistas of white sand and clear blue ocean, but most come for the wildlife. Rockhopper, gentoo, king, and Magellanic penguins waddle around the shorelines, while black-browed albatrosses soar overhead and cavort in rookery colonies around the island.

The highest concentration of wildlife is found at "the Neck," a narrow strip of land connecting two larger, elevated expanses. And while the birdlife tends to grab the limelight (hence the island's designation by BirdLife International as an Important Bird Area), elephant seals and other marine mammals, including sei whales and Peale's dolphins, have also been known to make an appearance.

Most people arrive on the Falkland Islands via cruise ships, but there are also some (infrequent) flights from Chile and the United Kingdom. There are more than 740 islands in total, though most are inaccessible.

IN FILM

Thanks to its seclusion and striking biodiversity, Saunders Island has been a backdrop for several nature documentaries, including *Penguins: Spy in the Huddle* (2013), *Deadly: Pole to Pole* (2013), *Planet Earth* (2006), and *National Geographic Explorer: Flying Devils* (2000).

A black-browed albatross grooms its chick in its nest on the Falkland Islands.

CUVERVILLE BEACH

A haven for penguins—and the occasional whale—surrounded by glaciers and mountains

CATEGORY: Wildlife   **BEST TIME TO GO:** November through March
WHAT YOU'LL EXPERIENCE: Gentoo penguin rookery, minke and humpback whales, Errera Channel

If you like your beaches icy and your penguins abundant, Antarctica's Cuverville Beach might just be your dream destination. Reaching it is a challenge, of course, as Cuverville is a small island tucked away at the entrance to the Errera Channel, which is about 620 miles (1,000 km) south of Patagonia's southern tip, across the Drake Passage. Cruise ships make the voyage and send their guests to the pebble-and-boulder beach in Zodiacs.

The island is surrounded by mountain peaks, glaciers, and icebergs. It's also mostly covered by a permanent ice cap.

Gentoo penguins have established colonies at both ends of the beach, as well as on higher ground behind it. As many as 7,000 breeding pairs have been counted here, making this the largest rookery of gentoo penguins on the Antarctic Peninsula. For this reason, along with the presence of terns, skuas, shags, and petrels, Cuverville has been declared an Important Bird Area by BirdLife International.

Marine mammals may also turn up during a visit. Several species of Antarctic seals, along with humpback and Antarctic minke whales, are sometimes spotted in the Errera Channel. In fact, this small island was once a commercial whaling hub, as evidenced by what's been left behind: a whaler's dam, abandoned whale bones, and discarded tools once used to haul whales in for processing.

HISTORY

Belgian explorer Adrien de Gerlache found his way to this approximately 1.2-by-1.5-mile (2-by-2.5-km) rock island in the late 1890s and named it after a vice admiral in the French navy, J.M.A. Cavelier de Cuverville.

Snow-topped mountains surround pebble-covered Cuverville Beach.

PART THREE
EUROPE

Castello Ruffo di Calabria stands guard over the beautiful seaside town of Scilla, Italy (page 198).

LUSKENTYRE BEACH

A white-sand beach ideal for canoeing and staring at the sea by a peat fire

CATEGORY: **Remote**   BEST TIME TO GO: **April through October; September for whales and dolphins**
WHAT YOU'LL EXPERIENCE: **Moors and machair, whales and dolphins, windsurfing, Atlantic Ocean**

On the Isle of Harris, in Scotland's exotic, far-flung Outer Hebrides, Luskentyre is a startling bay of white sand and blue-green sea. It's a place where wading into the unswimmably cold Atlantic brings refreshed delight (and shivers), and where the surroundings evoke Gaelic culture and history.

Even though the water is a bit chilly for an extended swim, many still don wet suits for windsurfing, canoeing, or stand-up paddleboarding on a calm day. Mostly, though, this is a place to do very little but walk and look and appreciate the tranquil beauty of the landscape.

Wild horses can be seen along the shore, while whales, several species of dolphins, and basking sharks are active along the coast, following their migration patterns.

On shore, the terrain is a mix of mountains and moorland—wide expanses of open shrubland, heavily dominated by purple-flowered heather. Closer to the beach, there's a rare low-lying grassland called machair, which means "fertile" in Gaelic; it's only found along the western coasts of Scotland and Ireland.

There are several first come, first served campgrounds nearby and a local outfit that rents vintage camper vans, perfect for spending a night or two on the water's edge with a peat fire to warm your sandy toes.

A WHALE OF A TRAIL

Harris is part of the Hebridean Whale Trail, a collection of 30 sites along Scotland's west coast that were selected to showcase low-impact whale-watching from the shore and encourage responsible viewing of the region's varied and abundant marine mammals.

The white sand of Luskentyre Beach glows in the morning sun.

TRAETH MWNT

A secluded bay beneath ancient sailors' "chapel of ease"

CATEGORY: Historical   **BEST TIME TO GO:** Mid-February through mid-October
WHAT YOU'LL EXPERIENCE: Dolphins, Welsh history, landmark hill, seal pups, Irish Sea

An ancient holy site with honey-colored sand, Traeth Mwnt (*traeth* is Welsh for "beach") in Cardigan, Wales, is tucked away in a small cove at the base of gently sloping concrete stairs, an easy walk with a view out across St. George's Channel toward Ireland. The area is known for the Church of the Holy Cross, a medieval sailors' "chapel of ease" (a parish for those remote or in transit) above the beach.

The beach is named for Foel y Mwnt, a 250-foot-tall (76 m) conical hill that's a local landmark. It's surrounded by grassy headlands and steep cliffs, which made it a protected stretch of sand for holy pilgrims to come ashore. The church, meanwhile, is believed to have been named for a large stone cross that once occupied the mount. The whitewashed 14th-century chapel is simply constructed but formidable, an ancient pilgrimage site where the bodies of saints were said to have stopped en route to burial at Bardsey Island, aka the Island of 20,000 Saints.

Today, the beach is best known as one of the region's most reliable places for spotting dolphins and small, white, fuzzy seal pups from August through December. Mostly, though, it's a pleasant place for families to visit the sea, enjoy an ice cream at the beach's refreshment stand, and take a stroll along a narrow trail along the deep green bluffs. Swimming is considered safe here, but there are no lifeguards on duty.

Grassy headlands and steep cliffs surround the cove of Traeth Mwnt.

DURDLE DOOR

An iconic limestone arch stands over one of the country's most beloved beaches.

CATEGORY: **Remote**   BEST TIME TO GO: **March through October**
WHAT YOU'LL EXPERIENCE: **Jurassic Coast, caves, tide pools, English Channel**

On Dorset's magnificent Jurassic Coast—a UNESCO World Heritage site along the southeastern shores of England—this beach and its namesake limestone arch are absolute showstoppers. The world-famous Durdle Door arch formed over millions of years by erosion caused by the crashing sea. Its fitting name comes from the Old English word *thirl*, meaning "to pierce, bore, or drill."

Visitors tend to gawk at the arch and nearby sea stacks, which are large columns of rock in the sea formed by erosion, and then move along. But it's also possible to camp, hike, explore nearby tide pools filled with crabs and seaweed, and swim (note that there are no lifeguards and conditions can get rough). Photographers love to visit in late December and early January, when the sun rises directly through the keyhole of the arch.

The easiest way to get to the beach is to drive to Durdle Door Holiday Park, or be dropped there by a public bus. (Note that on summer days the parking lot fills quickly.) From there, it's a 15-minute walk along a steep path of packed earth and gravel. Although the beach lies within a privately owned estate, much of it is accessible to the public. A one-mile (1.6 km) cliff walk between the beach and Lulworth Cove to the east is especially popular, as is the short detour down some steps to Man O'War Beach. From there, a visitor can view some caves at the base of chalk cliffs.

The Durdle Door is an accumulation of sedimentary rock that began piling up 140 million years ago during the Jurassic period.

PLAYA DE MIGJORN

The longest beach on the smallest island in Spain's Balearic Islands

CATEGORY: **Nature**   BEST TIME TO GO: **July through September**
WHAT YOU'LL EXPERIENCE: **Family-friendly swimming, nudists, historic lighthouses, Balearic Sea**

Playa de Migjorn (or Platja de Migjorn) takes its name from the Catalan word for "midday," a reference to its position as the sunniest beach on the Balearic island of Formentera. While this 3.7-mile (6 km) stretch of white sand has plenty to offer, from legendary beachside paella spots to atmospheric beach bars, it's remarkably undeveloped by the standards of this busy Spanish archipelago, which is also home to hot spots like Ibiza and Mallorca.

Formentera, the smallest of the Balearics, is only reachable by boat. Historically, that has given the island a bit of a counterculture, free-spirited, younger-sibling sensibility. On the south side of the island, between La Mola lighthouse and its main port, La Savina, lies Playa de Migjorn. Many of the beach's secluded stretches can be reached via dirt road offshoots from PM-820. Because the beach is so long, it's divided into four distinct sections: Ca Marí, near the village of Sant Ferran; Migjorn (the widest and most touristed); Es Arenals; and Es Copinar, near the scenic picturesque cove at Caló des Mort. Each has its own character.

South-facing Playa de Migjorn has calm sections with a soft, sandy bottom, perfect for families, while other sections have rocky outcroppings that offer privacy and are popular with nude bathers. In May through October, assisted swimming and beach wheelchairs are available for visitors with disabilities.

There is room to spread out on the miles-long beach of Playa de Migjorn.

SPIAGGIA DI SCILLA

A southern Italian beach that's home to a Greek myth and Calabrian tradition

CATEGORY: **Historical**   BEST TIME TO GO: **May through November**
WHAT YOU'LL EXPERIENCE: **Castello Ruffo, views of Sicily across the Strait of Messina, Tyrrhenian Sea**

I n the southern Italian province of Calabria, Scilla is less famous than nearby Tropea (and far less popular than the wildly overtouristed Amalfi Coast). But what Scilla lacks in star power, it makes up for in authenticity and deep historical roots.

Scilla is a charmingly traditional Italian fishing village where swordfish are still harpooned using ancient techniques, a ritual that's fascinating to watch from shore. The town clings to cliffs along the sparkling, deep-blue Tyrrhenian Sea, guarded by the Castello Ruffo di Calabria, which dates to the ancient Etruscans and dominates the coastline. After the Etruscans, the castle's walls were fortified by the Greeks during the period of Magna Graecia, then expanded further by the Romans. Today, the castle divides the town into two marinas (coasts, or neighborhoods): the beachfront Marina Grande; and Chianalea, the steep, tangled old town.

At the base of Marina Grande, Spiaggia di Scilla is a half-mile-long (800 m) beach of tan sand and smooth gray pebbles in the shadow of the ancient castle. The water is clear and clean, the lidos—beach bars that rent sun beds and umbrellas—are unpretentious, and the entire waterfront is uncrowded and family-friendly. Beachgoers also enjoy a view of the Strait of Messina, where the mythological monsters Charybdis and Scylla threatened seafarers, and the Aeolian Islands.

HISTORY

According to Greek mythology, a cave in Scilla is home to the female nymph Scylla, who was said to have 12 feet and six heads, three rows of vicious teeth, and a voracious appetite for anything—or anyone—in reach.

Spiaggia di Scilla has a family-friendly shoreline.

SPIAGGIA DEI CONIGLI

A remote Mediterranean beach off the coast of Africa that's home to loggerhead turtles

CATEGORY: Nature   **BEST TIME TO GO:** June through mid-July; September through October
WHAT YOU'LL EXPERIENCE: Powdery white sand, cream-and-tan cliffs, Mediterranean Sea

Lampedusa, part of the Pelagie Islands, is the southernmost point of Italy—much closer to Africa (86 miles/138 km away) than to Sicily (134 miles/215 km away). Yet it remains quintessentially Italian.

Lampedusa's most famous beach, Spiaggia dei Conigli, is named for the tiny islet just off its shore, Isola dei Conigli. *Conigli* is Italian for "rabbit," and it is sometimes known as Rabbit Island, but in fact, the island takes its name from the Arabic word *rabit*, which means something akin to "connection," referring to the fact that the islet is actually connected to the beach by a sandy isthmus that becomes visible at low tide.

Of Lampedusa's many stunning beaches in the south and cream-and-tan-colored cliffs along its northern coast, none is more breathtaking than Spiaggia dei Conigli, where the warm Mediterranean water fades from a pale turquoise to a deep blue and is wrapped in rust-colored headlands and vividly white, fine-grained sand. Shallow far from the shore, clear and clean, the sea here is eminently swimmable. As one of the island's most beloved attractions, the beach is protected from development and eyesores, such as beach chairs and umbrellas. Services, including bathrooms and a concession stand, are available at the parking area, about a 10-minute walk away.

Between mid-June and mid-October, admission to Spiaggia dei Conigli is limited to two daily shifts—either morning or afternoon—of 550 visitors each.

A HAVEN

As one of the closest European Union destinations to Tunisia, which is now the primary jumping-off point for those escaping wars and hardship across the Middle East and Africa, the eight-square-mile (21 km²) island has become one of the region's most significant havens for refugees and migrants in recent years.

The sun rises over the pristine beach at Spiaggia dei Conigli.

SPIAGGIA DI VIAREGGIO

Art Nouveau architecture and a famed Carnival draw locals to this beach town.

CATEGORY: Culture   **BEST TIME TO GO: June through October; February through March for Carnival**
WHAT YOU'LL EXPERIENCE: Historic *bagnos*, Carrara marble cliffs, Tyrrhenian Sea

n a nation of stunning beaches, Viareggio may not be the most postcard perfect. But it is one of Italy's earliest international beach destinations, known for its inordinately wide and 6.2-mile-long (10 km) coastline, backed by sand dunes in its wilder reaches. It's a belle epoque resort town with century-and-a-half-old beachfront hotels and restaurants that evoke a faded Art Nouveau grandeur.

While Tuscany remains one of Italy's most romanticized regions, today's tourists tend to head inland to Pisa, Florence, or the wine-soaked hills, saving their beachgoing for trendier, more social media–friendly shores. But Viareggio and the Versilia coast haven't fallen out of favor with Italians. They still crowd its oceanfront *bagnos*—private beach clubs that are called lidos elsewhere in the country—during the summer months. What Viareggio lacks in glamour, it makes up for in striking Art Nouveau architecture, local color, and unpretentiousness.

The town is also known for the celebrated Carnival of Viareggio, with its elaborate costumes and papier-mâché floats. Since 1873, it has been an annual event and is now considered among the most spectacular in Italy, second only perhaps to the Carnival of Venice. And the nearby mountains, with their Carrara marble quarries, shimmer in the distance, evoking a sort of timeless elegance.

A parade of floats floods the streets during the annual Carnival of Viareggio.

PLAGE DE PALOMBAGGIA

Surrounded by fragrant pines and red rocks, this small beach has a big reputation.

CATEGORY: Iconic   **BEST TIME TO GO: May through June; September**
WHAT YOU'LL EXPERIENCE: Blossoming maquis, Cerbicale Islands, Neptune grass forest, Mediterranean Sea

On the mountainous French island of Corsica, Plage de Palombaggia has plenty of competition as l'Île de Beauté's (the isle of beauty) most beautiful. With 620 miles (1,000 km) of coastline and some 200 beaches, Corsica is famous for its shoreline. But Palombaggia stands above the rest for its mile-long semicircle of fine white sand and red-hued rocks. It is so beloved that it's best to visit in the shoulder season.

The beach—about 6.5 miles (10.5 km) southwest of Porto-Vecchio and a short ferry ride from Sardinia, Italy—is in a small cove lined with umbrella pines in Bouches de Bonifacio Nature Reserve. In the spring, the island's dense, scented shrublands, known as maquis, are in bloom and the Mediterranean is beginning to warm, inviting snorkelers and swimmers into its turquoise and clear waters. The beach drops off gradually and lifeguards are on duty, making it a good swimming option for families, too. There are simple beach bars offering food and drink, along with lounge chair and umbrella rentals. Among the beach's few faults are a lack of shade and challenging parking.

To glimpse its underwater life, walk to the north end of the beach where two rocky points and a forest of Neptune grass offer sanctuary for octopuses, sea stars, and colorful fish, including painted combers and ornate and rainbow wrasse. But Palombaggia's real draw is its exaggerated beauty and dramatic vistas looking out across the Cerbicale Islands nature preserve.

A snorkeler explores the clear water off Palombaggia, where a forest of Neptune grass shelters abundant marine life.

D

OTHER NOTABLE BEACHES IN CORSICA

A PLAGE DE SANTA GIULIA: A short distance south of Palombaggia, Santa Giulia is a long, sandy peninsula that separates a lagoon—a stopover for flamingos in the winter—from the Mediterranean. The south-facing beach wraps around a shallow bay and is protected from the wind, making it popular with families, as well as paddle-boarders and kayakers.

B CAPO DI FENO: Watch surfers ride some of Corsica's biggest waves at Grand Capo and Petit Capo (aka Sevani), two beaches separated by a field just north of the Corsican capital of Ajaccio. In addition to surfing, the beach has a nude section and a *paillote*—a thatch-roofed beach restaurant—for enjoying an afternoon aperitif.

C PLAGES DE SALECCIA AND LOTU: These uncommonly undeveloped sister beaches are on a remote part of the island where Europe's only desert, the Désert des Agriates, meets the sea. They are only accessible by a small ferry from Saint-Florent or a 20-minute drive down a trail that's only suitable for four-wheel-drive vehicles.

D PLAGE DE CALVI: On the northern part of the island, Calvi's 3.7-mile (6 km) town beach has views of the city's medieval citadel, tangle of red-tiled roofs, and cobble-stone streets. Still, it's expansive enough to rarely feel overcrowded.

CALANQUE D'EN VAU

A dramatic cove carved from towering sea cliffs and brimming with marine life

CATEGORY: **Remote**　　BEST TIME TO GO: **March through November**

WHAT YOU'LL EXPERIENCE: **Cliffs, hiking trails, rock climbers, marine sanctuary, Mediterranean Sea**

Southeast of Marseille, France's majestic Parc National des Calanques is defined by a series of steep canyons, plunging valleys, and scenic coves carved out by wind and water over millennia (*calanque* is French for "rocky inlet"). And while these magnificent landforms only got their due as a national park in 2012, the poster beach for all this unspeakable beauty—Calanque d'En Vau—has been wildly popular for decades.

The trip to this beach starts in Cassis, a historic fishing village circled by vineyards and olive groves. Most visitors access the beach via a rugged trail from the Presqu'île de Cassis parking lot over the white-and-gray cliffs, which takes two to three hours round-trip (not including a dip in the sea). The path is challenging, with incredibly steep descents, but some beachgoers insist on making things even more difficult by rock climbing up and down the limestone cliffs. Other adventurers choose to make their way to Calanque d'En Vau by boat tours or kayak journeys (either guided or self-led).

The national park protects nearly 200 square miles (520 km²) of land and sea, including the Calanques (unique limestone coves that cut inland, forming steep, narrow valleys by the Mediterranean Sea) and a marine sanctuary beneath the surface. The vivid blue water is cool, and snorkelers and divers glide among octopuses, anemones, and a wide variety of fish. Dives are done from boat tours, but you can snorkel right from the shore.

OPPOSITE: **A hiker overlooks the cool waters of Calanque d'En Vau.**

PAGES 210-211: **Kayakers in Calanque d'En Vau are able to explore coves not seen from the coast.**

The beach gets crowded in summertime, so arrive early to find a good spot in the pebbles for your towel. There are no facilities at the beach; be sure to bring along plenty of water, snacks, picnic supplies, and whatever else you might need. In the middle of the day there's no shade, so get ready to soak up the sun.

If you have more time, it's worth setting out on the park's many hiking trails to visit some of its other beaches. The tourist office in Cassis offers free trail maps.

NEARBY BEACHES

CALANQUE DE PORT PIN: On the hike from the parking lot to Calanque d'En Vau, you'll go right by this beach— a sand-and-pebble stunner with clear blue water that reflects the blues of the sky and the greens of the surrounding Aleppo pines. There's a steep, rocky descent to get to the beach.

CALANQUE DE MARSEILLEVEYRE: A farther-flung gem at the southwestern end of the national park, Calanque de Marseilleveyre is accessed by a 45-minute hike from the Port de Callelongue. Highlights include views of the vast Mediterranean, plunging cliffs, and a series of mini calanques. You can also arrive by sea kayak.

BEACH HIKES

Traversing coastlines by foot rewards intrepid hikers with stunning views and isolated beaches.

A long-distance hike along a coastline is a spectacular thing. You can count on captivating ocean views, blissful solitude, and the soothing sounds of waves crashing—or even better, pebbles tumbling over one another—*wssssssssh*. The tide often brings in surprises, and with remote beaches accessible only by foot, your chance of being the one to stumble upon those surprises is maximized. Few of life's pleasures rival the simple act of drifting off to sleep in a tent near the sea, then rising with the sun for a stroll in the sand. Just ask anyone who's slept on Kalalau Beach in Kauai, which is reached only via a grueling but gobsmackingly beautiful 11-mile (18 km) cliffside hike.

There are, of course, some special considerations when hiking for a long time on sand and near the sea. You'll need extra water, and sunscreen is obviously essential (make it the reef-safe stuff if you plan on snorkeling). The importance of choosing correct footwear cannot be overstated. Invest in a pair of sturdy hiking boots that will keep sand out and feet dry, and break them in before your hike. Also, beware the impact of hot sand on shoes over time, and carry glue or tape for repairs.

Finally, pay attention to the water itself. For example, on one of the world's most famous beach hikes—the northern section of the Lost Coast Trail, which covers 24.6 miles (39.6 km) of California coastal wilderness—hikers must mind

The Nā Pali Coast offers a gorgeous beach hike along the Kalalau Trail near Hanakapi'ai Beach, Kauai, Hawaii.

the tides; bad timing can trap them between steep cliffs and an incoming sea. Whatever you do while hiking a beach, never turn your back on the ocean—especially when weighted down by a backpack.

NOTABLE BEACH HIKES AROUND THE WORLD

A KALALAU TRAIL, NĀ PALI COAST, KAUAI, HAWAII, U.S.A.: The 11-mile (18 km) trail traverses cliffs and five valleys before ending at Kalalau Beach.

B WEST COAST TRAIL, VANCOUVER ISLAND, BRITISH COLUMBIA, CANADA: Vancouver Island's iconic 47-mile (75 km) coastal trail requires hiking across white-sand beaches and through forests, and climbing ladders.

C PLAYA DEL RISCO, ISLA GRACIOSA, CANARY ISLANDS, SPAIN: This short 4.7-mile (7.5 km) round-trip hike begins near the village of Ye and descends a steep path past a salt-making lagoon to the remote beach of Playa del Risco, which has white sand and vibrant blue 70°F (21°C) water.

D ABEL TASMAN COAST TRACK, SOUTH ISLAND, NEW ZEALAND: Winding through dense forest and over graham cracker–colored sand, this 37-mile (60 km) hike hugs the coast within an eponymous national park.

E WALES COAST PATH, WALES, UNITED KINGDOM: The mother of all beach hikes opened in 2012, stretching a whopping 870 miles (1,400 km) across the entirety of the Welsh coastline. There are *so many* castles.

HUNDSTRAND ROTES KLIFF BEACH

A windswept island beach at the foot of the gorgeous Rotes Kliff

CATEGORY: Culture   **BEST TIME TO GO:** Late May through early September
WHAT YOU'LL EXPERIENCE: *Strandkorbs,* Michelin-starred restaurants, views of Denmark, North Sea

The tiny Frisian island of Sylt, the northernmost point of Germany, may seem like an unexpected beach getaway. But this sliver of a windswept island offers a coastline that features sand dunes and imposing cliffs, swaying reeds and mudflats, cycling routes and bird-watching, and 25 miles (40 km) of beaches. In recent years, the island's historic 17th- and 18th-century homes—many once belonging to whaling captains—were joined by luxury hotels and several Michelin-starred restaurants, earning Sylt a reputation as a posh getaway for the European elite.

The temperature here rarely gets much above 70°F (21°C) and the island's suboceanic climate is often wet and rainy. Still, the beaches—lined with distinctive big, boxy, blue-and-white-striped hooded windbreak chairs, known as *strandkorbs*—draw crowds to the island's uncommonly atmospheric coastline.

On Sylt's west coast, Hundstrand Rotes Kliff (Red Cliffs Beach) is distinguished by its striking, 98-foot-high (30 m) rusty-hued cliff face, which traditionally served as a navigational aid for passing boats and remains the beach's defining feature. Walk the beach between Wenningstedt and Kampen villages for a view of the cliffs from below, or climb the wooden steps to the top of the 172-foot (52 m) Uwe Dune, which is Sylt's highest point and offers spectacular views of the coastline and nearby islands.

Leuchtturm List-Ost, built in 1857, is found in the beach grass–covered dunes on the island of Sylt.

POTAMI BEACH

A pebbled beach that's near waterfalls, ancient churches, and a Genoan fortress

CATEGORY: Historical   **BEST TIME TO GO:** June through September
WHAT YOU'LL EXPERIENCE: Less-visited Greek island, Greek mythological sites, Aegean Sea

Closer to Turkey than it is to mainland Greece, Sámos is a bit apart from the usual stops on the Mediterranean tourist circuit. Said to be home to the goddess Hera, the great mathematician Pythagoras, and the philosopher Epicurus, the island has a distinguished reputation as a place of intellectual and mythological might. But even cultural tourists who come for Sámos's two UNESCO monuments—the remains of the fortified city of Pythagoreion and the Temple of Hera—may want to retreat to the shade of an umbrella on the sundeck at the beautiful Potami Beach, where restaurants rent lounge chairs and offer cold drinks and beach snacks.

On Sámos's northern coast, just over a mile (2 km) from Karlovasi, Potami sits among cliffs and pines and is fronted by crystalline cobalt blue water. The blue flag beach, which means it is recognized for exceptional cleanliness, is covered in small, smooth stones perfect for those who dislike how sand clings to the body. The water quality makes for fine snorkeling, especially when the winds cooperate.

Many visitors to Potami combine their time at the beach with a short hike into the surrounding hills, where there's a 13th-century Genoan castle and the 11th-century Metamorfosis Sotiros. On the way back, in a narrow canyon less than a quarter mile (350 m) inland from the shore, the Potami waterfalls and pools make for a refreshing dip before you return to the beach.

Rocky slopes surround the pebble beach of Potami.

ERESSOS, LÉSVOS, GREECE

SKALA ERESSOS

A beach town that celebrates Sapphic romance and New Age counterculture

CATEGORY: **Culture**   BEST TIME TO GO: **May through October**
WHAT YOU'LL EXPERIENCE: **Ouzo distilleries, beachside tavernas, women's festival, Aegean Sea**

Lésvos (aka Lesbos), Greece's third largest island, is a cultured destination filled with deep and compelling history. It has a prominent university and the internationally known Tériade Museum, which celebrates modern artists from Greece and around the world, and the city of Mytilene serves as the capital of the North Aegean region. Known for its ouzo—the traditional Greek anise-flavored spirit; half the world's supply is produced here—and "liquid gold" (aka olive oil), Lésvos's economy is still largely agricultural. And, unusual for a Greek island, Lésvos remains relatively non-touristy, its gorgeous beaches uncrowded. Some, like Skala Eressos, have a distinctive culture of their own.

Eressos, on the south coast, is an idiosyncratic beach town with a pebble shore and clean, clear water backed by charming tavernas that rent beach chairs and deliver cold drinks for a modest price. The town is said to be either the birthplace or onetime home of Sappho, the lyric poet who lived in the sixth century B.C. and remains one of the best-known writers in history. Since the 1970s, Skala Eressos has attracted female travelers inspired by the poet's evocative depictions of love between women. There's an impressive statue of Sappho on the beach's promenade, and each September the town holds a women's festival featuring everything from ecstatic dance to guided mountain biking to film screenings.

OPPOSITE: Visitors enjoy cocktails with a view of the Aegean Sea.

PAGES 222-223: On Lésvos, grilled octopus is often served with ouzo, which is produced on the island.

The beach town has a history of attracting free spirits, including the prominent Indian mystic Bhagwan Shree Rajneesh (aka Osho, who died in 1990) and his New Age devotees. To cater to his followers, Eressos has a large number of vegetarian restaurants, yoga and massage studios, and an overall sense that this isn't your typical Greek village.

OTHER LÉSVOS BEACHES

AGIOS ISIDOROS BEACH: On Lésvos's southern coast, the fishing community of Plomari is famous for being the center of ouzo production and for its fine waterfront tavernas at which to enjoy it. A half-hour walk from Plomari, the village of Agios Isidoros is known for two things: its exceptionally clean beach, which is considered among the most beautiful on the island, and Varvayanni, a family-operated distillery that has been making ouzo since 1860. The distillery operates a museum of ouzo and offers tours and tastings.

PARALIA SIGRI: On the far western edge of Lésvos, the village of Sigri is out of the way even by Lésvos standards. The town's beach is sheltered by tiny Nissiopi Island just offshore, creating an unusually calm swimming beach. Nissiopi is known for its petrified forest, viewed along gentle trails at the Marine Park of Nissiopi, which is a UNESCO Global Geopark, and a museum of natural history that is devoted to it. Combine the two for a great day trip.

PARALIA AGIOS ERMOGENIS: Not far south of the Lésvos capital of Mytilene at the mouth of the Gulf of Gera, there's a dead-end road. Follow it to a cove of pines with two stretches of sand and pebbles divided by a wall of rock with a view of the beach's white-and-blue-domed chapel.

ELAFONISI BEACH

Ringing a lagoon, this pink-sand beach and its offshore island have a sad history.

CATEGORY: **Nature**   BEST TIME TO GO: **Fall or winter**
WHAT YOU'LL EXPERIENCE: **Clear water, nature preserve, local tavernas, Mediterranean Sea**

At the southwest corner of Crete, between the coastal villages of Moni Chrisoskalitissis and Gialos, Elafonisi Beach is best known for its exotic expanse of pink-hued sand and clear turquoise lagoon. Its distinctive color, like other pink-sand beaches around the world (page 309), is the product of foraminifera, a single-celled microorganism with a reddish shell.

A short distance across the lagoon is the small, uninhabited Elafonisi Island; the sea is so shallow that you can walk from one island to the other. Elafonisi Island (*elafonisi* is Greek for "deer") is a nature preserve as part of the European Union's Natura 2000 protected area program. It's notable both for its photogenic setting and its tragic history. In 1907, dozens of passengers died off its coast (and were later buried ashore) when the Austrian ship *Imperatrix* sank and its lifeboat did not make it ashore. Both the shipwreck and the grave sites remain.

Elafonisi Island's sad past is now distant enough to have become part of regional lore, only adding to Elafonisi Beach's allure. Visitors are captivated by the beach's striking colors of pink and bright blue, rolling dunes, and dramatic mountains. In the summer, the shore is crowded with beach chairs and umbrellas, as it's a popular weekend getaway for residents of Chania, Crete's main city. A few hours in the sun here are best followed up with a seafood dinner and some Greek wine at a nearby taverna.

The pink sand in the lagoon of Elafonisi Beach makes it a popular getaway for residents of nearby Chania.

ZLATNI RAT BEACH

A decadent tendril of pebbles and sand jutting into the Adriatic Sea

CATEGORY: Remote   **BEST TIME TO GO:** May through October
WHAT YOU'LL EXPERIENCE: Finger-shaped beach, snorkeling, wind sports, Adriatic Sea

This famous finger of Croatian sand is officially called Zlatni Rat Beach, but visitors tend to use the translations: Golden Horn or Golden Cape. The beach's peculiar shape has led to its protection in Croatia as a geomorphological monument, even as it serves as a magnet for international travelers. Essentially, Zlatni is a large, pebble-strewn spit of beach surrounded by clear blue water, backed by Mediterranean pine trees, and filled with as many as 10,000 visitors on a busy day.

The beach juts into the Adriatic Sea from the southern end of Brač island, which is in the Dalmatia region. It is easily accessed via ferry or boat tour from Split or Trogir. From the island's main village, Bol, it is about a half hour's walk along a pathway through the pine forest. Those who don't want to walk can hop on a quick boat taxi. A beach towel and a snorkel are highly recommended, as grouper, wrasse, octopus, and other sea creatures regularly make appearances. Wind sports enthusiasts can get their thrills when the breeze picks up in the afternoon.

Thanks to all the wind, tides, and current along this coast, the tendril-like, double-sided beach changes shape throughout the year. Sometimes the tip rotates into a curl, bending either to the east or the west. Other times, a small pool forms at the end. No matter when you go, at least one side of the beach will offer calm conditions ideal for children (and adults!) to wade and frolic.

The double-sided pebble beach in Bol changes shape with the seasons.

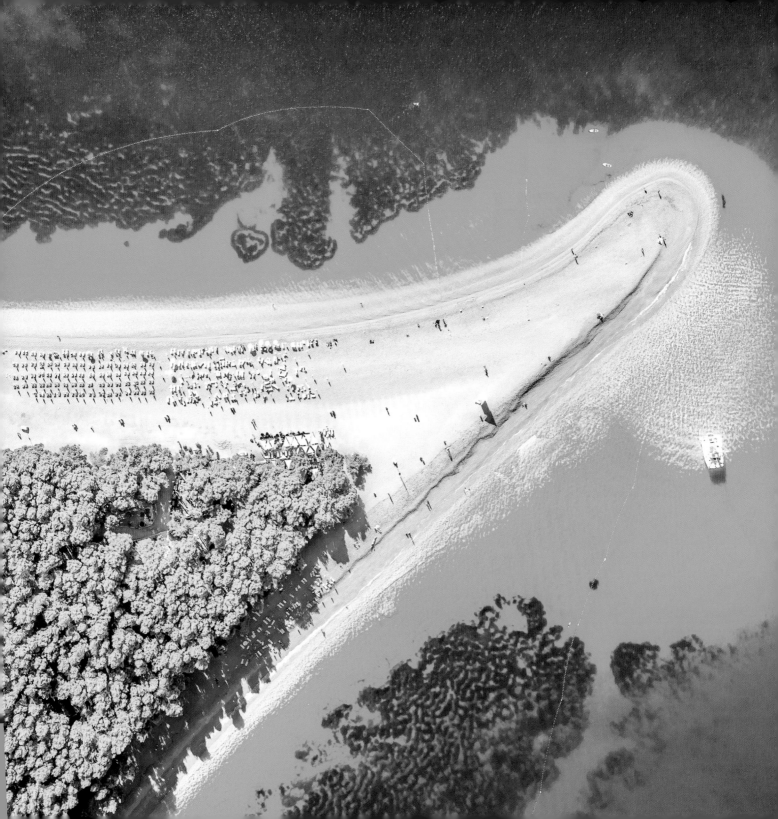

SVETI STEFAN BEACH

Pink-sand beaches form a narrow isthmus that leads to a centuries-old village.

CATEGORY: Historical   **BEST TIME TO GO:** June through August
WHAT YOU'LL EXPERIENCE: Historic royal villa, olive grove–covered hillsides, Adriatic Sea

On the coast of Montenegro between Budva and Bar, the fortified village of Sveti Stefan is a dramatic sight: a tight cluster of 500-year-old stone villas hanging over the deep blue Adriatic. A so-called tombolo, or tethered island, Sveti Stefan is connected to the coast via a narrow constructed isthmus—forming a double-sided beach that's a mix of pink sand and pebbles. The beach is known as Ivano Vidoni Beach on one side and Sveti Stefan Plaža 2 on the other.

The island was a strategically important fortress beginning in the 1400s, built to defend the coastline against the Turks. Later, in the 1800s, locals began living on it, and by the 1930s the Serbian royal family had built a summer home here. After World War II, the communist Yugoslav government deposed the royal family and nationalized the island fortress. Residents were moved to the mainland and Sveti Stefan was developed into a high-end resort that hosted celebrities such as Marilyn Monroe, Sophia Loren, Kirk Douglas, and Elizabeth Taylor from the 1960s into the 1980s, before becoming run-down and falling out of fashion.

In 2007, after the breakup of Yugoslavia, the new country of Montenegro leased the entire island of Sveti Stefan to a high-end hospitality company and the historic village was restored, once again, as a luxury hotel. Sveti Stefan is only accessible to guests of the resort, who are shuttled there via speedboat,

OPPOSITE: Chaise longues line Sveti Stefan Plaža 2 on the beachside road up to the resort.

PAGES 230-231: The twinkling lights of Sveti Stefan sparkle at sunset against the Adriatic Sea.

> *"Just as if I have returned to town from the most beautiful fairy tale of my childhood."*
> —SOPHIA LOREN, ITALIAN ACTRESS

helicopter, or Mercedes-Benz. But while the island is off-limits to the public, much of Sveti Stefan Beach remains free to access—though there is a section reserved for hotel guests or those willing to shell out $110 for a day-use fee to sunbathe alongside the rich and famous. The water is deep near the beach and has an average temperature of 78°F (25.5°C), making it ideal for swimming.

The resort also owns nearby Queen's Beach, which is home to Villa Miločer, the former summertime retreat of Queen Maria of Yugoslavia, and Miločer Beach, one bay south, which is sometimes called King's Beach because it was favored by Queen Maria's husband, King Alexander. Surrounded by cliffs, forests, and acres of olive trees, Queen's Beach is only accessible by boat and, until 2023, could only be visited by guests of the Sveti Stefan resort. But, after facing a backlash, the government reached a compromise with the company and the beach can again be visited by the public for a hefty fee.

PRAIA DA MARINHA

A sheer sandstone dream on the Atlantic, with a famous M-shaped arch

CATEGORY: **Remote**   BEST TIME TO GO: **June through August**
WHAT YOU'LL EXPERIENCE: **Clear water, sea stacks, soft sand, Atlantic Ocean**

This dramatic stretch of Algarve's shore ranks among the world's most dazzling coastlines. Its soaring sandstone cliffs, arches, and pillars appear in stacks of promotional materials for the region, so the staggering number of tourists that descend, particularly in summertime, is unsurprising. But it's worth dealing with the crowds to experience this striking beauty.

You'll need a car to reach the area, which is a 4.5-mile (7 km) drive from the town of Lagoa. There's ample parking atop a nearby cliff, but arriving in the early morning is the best way to guarantee you get a spot. Visitors set out along a walking trail over the cliffs, enjoying panoramic views of distinctive sandstone formations, including the famous M rock—essentially a double arch that looks like, you guessed it, the letter *M*. It's also known as Cathedral.

After taking in the views and snapping photos, descend the long stairway to the beach, where there's a restaurant on the soft, tan sand, and a rather large rock. Walk around the rock (and pay attention to the ocean, as high tide can make this tricky) and you'll find a larger expanse of sand on the other side. When you've had your fill of baking in the sun, you'll find the water cool and usually ideal for snorkeling, though conditions can occasionally become rough. Those interested in exploring sea caves can hop on boat tours from nearby Praia de Benagil (a 45-minute walk from Praia da Marinha).

The distinctive sandstone formations off the coast of Praia da Marinha can be viewed from a trail over the cliffs.

ILHÉU DE VILA FRANCA

A sliver of sand in the caldera of a sunken volcano

CATEGORY: Unusual   **BEST TIME TO GO:** June through October
WHAT YOU'LL EXPERIENCE: Birds, cliff diving, dragon tree, Azorean flowers, Atlantic Ocean

Just over a mile (1.6 km) off the south-central coast of São Miguel in the Portuguese Azores, Ilhéu de Vila Franca is a volcanic crater with a round, strikingly blue natural swimming pool at its center. Uninhabited, the entire island is a nature preserve. Only 4,000 years old—considered young in geological time—the island receives a steady stream of visitors, mostly via frequent ferry service, which runs from June through October, from the nearby town of Vila Franca do Campo.

The island's appeal, beyond the novelty of swimming in the caldera of an extinct volcano, is its plethora of birds and wildlife. When the tide is right, visitors can lay a towel on a thin sliver of a sandy beach, although there is very little shade. Visitors are encouraged to bring everything they will need, as there is nothing for sale in the nature preserve. It's also a destination for cliff divers. There are two platforms on the island's highest cliff face—at 69 and 89 feet (21 and 27 m) above the ocean—that are used for international competitions.

The islet's lagoon is almost entirely separated from the surrounding Atlantic Ocean by volcanic slopes—rocky and topped with Azorean flowers, abandoned vineyards, and an impressive dragon tree. There is an opening, called the Boquete, that faces north and so keeps out the ocean waves, making for a calm shelter inside the lagoon.

Ilhéu de Vila Franca was created by an underwater volcano and shaped by the sea.

VÍK Í MÝRDAL, ICELAND

REYNISFJARA BEACH

Iceland's famous black-sand stunner features basalt stacks and colossal waves.

CATEGORY: Nature   BEST TIME TO GO: Year-round
WHAT YOU'LL EXPERIENCE: Sea stacks, puffins, sneaker waves, sea caves, Atlantic Ocean

Of all the black-sand beaches in Iceland—and there are many—Reynisfjara stands out as the most enchanting. (Case in point: It was chosen as a backdrop for season seven of the HBO series *Game of Thrones*.) Its unique basalt formations and peculiar sea stacks, known locally as Reynisdrangar, loom large in Icelandic folklore, and a jaunt along this revered shore is rounded out with sightings of puffins, forays into sea caves, and wave action at its finest. Just be sure not to turn your back on the ocean; Reynisfjara is as famous for its beguiling beauty as it is for its ruthless sneaker waves (a surprisingly large wave that can appear without warning), which have taken the lives of several unlucky tourists.

The moody beach lies about 112 miles (180 km) southeast of Reykjavik, near a small fishing village called Vík í Mýrdal. Most travelers drive to the beach on their own, but it's also possible to visit this beach, and other sites on Iceland's south coast, as part of a guided tour. Sunrise and sunset are the best times to make it here if you want to avoid crowds and get a great photo. But you should also plan around low tide, which allows for the opportunity to peer into sea caves and see the basalt columns without fear of those massive sneaker waves crashing in.

Jutting out of the sea just offshore, the bizarre Reynisdrangar columns are at the center of several local legends. One story claims that several trolls

The aurora borealis reflects off the water surrounding the basalt rock stack known as Hvítserkur.

made the mistake of attempting to push ships to shore late in the evening. When dawn broke and they had not yet succeeded, the trolls perished. The columns are said to be their petrified remains. Another myth says they are the remains of an ancient, grounded ship. But if science is to be believed, the basalt columns were formed by cooling hot lava. The black-sand beach is made of the same stuff, shattered into tiny fragments and broken down into fine particles by erosion.

Other natural attractions in the area include Atlantic puffins, which nest on the mountain cliffs surrounding the beach. These highly charismatic black-and-white seabirds sport multicolored bills and are famous for stuffing said beaks with a variety of small fish. Bird-watchers will also appreciate catching glimpses of fulmars and guillemots.

Don't get so distracted by the scenery and the wildlife that you forget to keep an eye on the sea. Sneaker waves pound this shoreline with alarming fury. There is essentially nothing between Reynisfjara and Antarctica, which is what gives those waves thousands of miles to build. The tallest waves have been as high as a 10-story building. And you never know when one will strike. Visitors have been soaked, knocked off their feet, and even taken out to sea by rip currents on more than a few occasions. There have been at least five deaths at the beach, all occurring within the last decade. Do not attempt swimming here.

The key is to always watch the waves, keep a safe distance, and don't turn your back even for a minute. Pay attention to any warnings from local authorities; at times, a yellow or red light may be displayed, which is a signal to visitors not to travel beyond the light. There are no lifeguards or security measures of any kind, in part because rescues would be too dangerous. Rockfalls and rockslides are also a concern beneath the steep, unstable cliffs on the eastern part of the beach. With great beauty often comes great danger—but in this case it's worth it.

Legend has it that these basalt columns were once trolls who turned to stone in the sunlight.

OTHER NOTABLE ICELANDIC BEACHES

DJÚPALÓNSSANDUR BEACH: On the Snæfellsnes Peninsula in western Iceland, this former fishing village is famous for black volcanic sand, jagged rock formations, and remnants of a shipwreck. Sneaker waves can sneak up in Djúpalónssandur too, so take care.

SKARÐSVÍK BEACH: On the northwestern tip of the Snæfellsnes Peninsula, this beach stands out for its golden sand and turquoise water—a rare sight in Iceland. It's also surrounded by cliffs and lava formations.

DIAMOND BEACH: Glittering remnants of icebergs washed ashore from the Jökulsárlón Glacier Lagoon sparkle on the black sand. The beach is an important breeding ground for the arctic tern and the great skua, and orcas are often spotted offshore.

ABOVE: Chunks of ice from the Breiðamerkurjökull glacier glow against the black sand of Diamond Beach.

OPPOSITE: Black basalt sea caves that line Reynisfjara are accessible at low tide.

HAUKLAND BEACH

The scenic vistas of this Arctic beach can be enjoyed from both land and sea.

CATEGORY: Remote   **BEST TIME TO GO: June through September**
WHAT YOU'LL EXPERIENCE: Midnight sun, Arctic Circle, Mannen Peak, Norwegian Sea

Off the northwestern coast of Norway, Lofoten is an Arctic archipelago—not the typical place people look for beaches. Sitting just above the Arctic Circle, at 68° north latitude, this majestic, mountainous landscape is better known for the northern lights, midnight sun, ski touring, and Trollfjord excursions than it is for sandy bays.

But during the warmest months (June through September), when the frost has thawed, Vestvågøya Island's Haukland Beach—a moon-shaped stretch of sand around a deep blue-and-turquoise, remarkably clear bay backed by lush green grass—looks deceptively tropical. The early summer (roughly late May through mid-July) coincides with the island's brief window of midnight sun, when the sun does not set at all and there is light 24 hours of the day. Enjoy a night under the sun at one of the waterfront camping sites.

For the four warm months of the year, the beach, which takes its name from the working farm that surrounds it, becomes an outdoorsy destination. The valley opens to dispersed camping (in designated areas), and paddleboards, kayaks, and wet suits are available for rent from the beach's concession stand. Hiking trails to nearby Uttakleiv Beach and Mannen Peak offer the challenge of a strenuous trek with the reward of a breathtaking view.

While tourists flock to Haukland in the summer months, sunset is just as lovely in the winter.

FRIGID BEACHES

While not ideal for swimming, these stunning beaches offer travelers wonders worth the trip.

Just because a beach isn't made for sunbathing and bodysurfing doesn't mean it doesn't have its charms. Even notoriously chilly places like Antarctica, Norway, and northern Japan (Omori-hama Beach, Hokkaido) have beautiful and fascinating shores. These are microclimates where sand and sea meet snow and ice, where white-capped mountains meet the crystalline shore of a frozen lake, and where frosty conditions create unusual phenomena.

Among these phenomena is the visually striking pancake ice that forms along the coasts of the Great Lakes in the United States. These semicircular, flat, mini-icebergs require the right temperature (just below freezing) and motion (wave action along the shore) to create their distinctive shapes, which crowd together at the surface and jostle in the windswept, partially frozen water.

In Finland in 2019, a rarer and more dramatic phenomenon occurred: An entire beach on Hailuoto Island was covered in nearly spherical balls of ice—some said to be as large as soccer balls—created by a process in which small pieces of ice were rolled through the near-freezing water by intense wind. Don't let the cold keep you away from the coast. There is beauty to be found even when you are bundled up, everything from glaciers to hot springs. Here are some other notable cold-weather beaches around the world.

The northern lights are visible eight months a year on the beaches of the Lofoten Islands in Norway.

OTHER NOTABLE FRIGID BEACHES

A SKAGEN, DENMARK: On the northern tip of Jutland in Denmark is the sandy Skagen Odde peninsula, a sandbar spit where the Baltic and North Seas meet.

B WHALERS BAY, DECEPTION ISLAND, ANTARCTICA: Once a whaling port, this volcanic island beach is now home to endangered Antarctic fur seals. Kroner Lake, a geothermally heated lagoon, is on the western side of the bay.

C BATUMI BEACH, BATUMI, GEORGIA: Miles of pebbles cover Batumi Beach, where the port city meets the Black Sea. The palm-shaded promenade typically draws summertime tourists, but the resort city also sees occasional snow—creating the striking sight of frosted palm fronds along the Black Sea coast.

D SHIKINE-JIMA, NI-JIMA, JAPAN: On this volcanic island near Tokyo, winter visitors can warm up in natural hot springs, known as *onsen*, along the coast.

E CHARMOUTH, DORSET, ENGLAND, UNITED KINGDOM: Winter is an ideal time to go fossil hunting on Dorset's Jurassic Coast. Landslides from the surrounding cliffs uncover fossils that include ammonites, belemnites, and, for the lucky few, an ichthyosaur.

F LAKE NAHUEL HUAPÍ, BARILOCHE, ARGENTINA: The northern Patagonian town is a destination for everything from kitesurfing to scuba diving to skiing, with views of the snowcapped peaks of the Andes. The glacial Lake Nahuel Huapí, with intensely clear blue waters, is one of the largest in the region and has several scenic alpine beaches of sand and pebbles.

PART FOUR
AFRICA

The striking Anse Source d'Argent on
La Digue island in Seychelles may well
be one of the most photographed
beaches in the world (page 292).

GRAND-POPO BEACH

The beach that celebrates the birthplace of vodun spiritual traditions

CATEGORY: **Culture**   BEST TIME TO GO: **January**
WHAT YOU'LL EXPERIENCE: **Mono Transboundary Biosphere Reserve, sea turtles, Gulf of Guinea**

Every year on January 10, the West African country of Benin celebrates the Fête du Vaudou on the long beach of Grand-Popo, part of a fishing village on the border with Togo. Benin is considered the cradle of vodun, and its annual festival is a national holiday. The celebration honors one of the world's most misunderstood religions: vodun, the animist religion from which new-world voodoo traditions evolved. Vodun is rooted in the belief that everything in the natural world, from trees to stones, has a spirit.

During the festival, thousands of vodun priests and practitioners, as well as curious tourists, arrive in Grand-Popo, which sits at the mouth of the Mono River and has an expansive but unswimmable beach. Celebrations include the ritual slaughter of a goat, processions in pirogues (dugout canoes), the use of fetishes (objects believed to have supernatural powers to communicate with spirits), elaborate masks, singing, dancing, and drinking gin.

The beach here is a long, wide strip of sand that separates the Bight of Benin (a bay in the Gulf of Guinea) from the Grand-Popo Lagoon. The lagoon is at the mouth of the Mono River, an area known as *la bouche du roi* ("the mouth of the king"), and it has a tragic history. The Mono was a significant route for transporting enslaved people. Though the interconnected lagoons of Benin's coast extend nearly the width of this tiny country, Grand-Popo has one of the few outlets to the sea, which made it a major port for the transatlantic

OPPOSITE: **A woman on Grand-Popo Beach carries fresh fish.**

PAGES 252-253: **Dancers spin at the Fête du Vaudou in Benin.**

slave trade. The nearby city of Ouidah, which is the unofficial capital of vodun culture, was a Portuguese fort during the slave trade, has museums and the Door of No Return monument dedicated to this area's tragic history.

Today, Grand-Popo has made a name for itself in another way: It is best known as a low-key vacation stopover between Lomé, Togo, and Benin's largest city, Cotonou. With welcoming, affordable guesthouses lining the beach, the small city—really a collection of 44 villages—is a base for experiencing the Mono Transboundary Biosphere Reserve, which protects 856,000 acres (346,300 ha) of forest and coastal wetlands in Benin, Togo, and Ghana, along with an endangered population of hippopotamus.

The beach here is a long, wide swath of deep golden-orange sand backed by thatched shade structures and palms. The nicer waterfront hotels have pools, as this stretch of Atlantic coast is notoriously dangerous and rip currents make ocean swimming an at-your-own-risk activity. But there's more to do here than laze on the sand, watching the ocean from a hammock. It's possible to tour the lagoon and its mangrove forests in a pirogue or to visit the local palm wine– and salt-making communities to see the traditional production processes. January 8 is the annual sea turtle conservation awareness day in Benin, dedicated to the preservation of endangered hawksbill, leatherback, and olive ridley sea turtles. On that day, hatcheries can be visited and babies are released.

BLUE LAGOON

A remote lagoon beach at the foot of the Sinai mountains

CATEGORY: Sport-centric   **BEST TIME TO GO:** November through February
WHAT YOU'LL EXPERIENCE: Ras Abu Galum nature reserve, Blue Hole, wind sports, Red Sea

The Blue Lagoon is a hook-shaped semispiral of golden sand and shallow turquoise water on the Red Sea coast of Egypt's Sinai Peninsula. The beach is so remote that it takes a taxi, a boat, and a four-wheel-drive vehicle, plus a hike along a seaside trail—or an entertaining camel ride—to reach it. From the nearest town, the coastal village of Dahab, it's an easy yet adventurous day trip.

Within the Ras Abu Galum Protectorate, a nature reserve famous for its exceptional diving, the Blue Lagoon is the place to experience sparse desert beauty away from the resorts and crowds that are common in Egyptian beach towns like Sharm el-Sheikh and Hurghada. The undeveloped lagoon sits at the foot of the striking red-and-brown Sinai mountains and is lined with rustic beach shacks made of reeds, where you'll find food and shade. The reserve itself protects 154 square miles (400 km²) of coastline and is a destination for wind sports—windsurfing historically, and kiteboarding more recently. The lagoon has a shallow, sandy bottom and is protected from the sea, so even when it's windy, it remains a veritable swimming pool—a stark contrast to the open water beyond its mouth.

Any trip to the Blue Lagoon starts with a stop at the Blue Hole—a 328-foot-deep (100 m) submarine sinkhole that's famous among free divers. From there, it's a scenic three-mile (5 km) coastal walk or a short boat ride to the

OPPOSITE: A combination of perfect wind and calm waters makes the Blue Lagoon on the Red Sea an ideal windsurfing destination.

PAGES 256-257: Sun loungers line the rock-and-sand Red Sea beach at Dahab Lagoon Resort.

Bedouin village of Ras Abu Galum, the ideal stop for a traditional lunch of fresh-caught fish and Bedouin tea made from cardamom, cinnamon, dried wild sage, black tea, and sugar. The snorkeling along the coast between Dahab and the Blue Lagoon is fantastic, with vibrant coral reefs, shoals of colorful fish, as well as turtles, and eagle and manta rays. Gear can be rented at the Blue Hole and, if one day isn't enough, beach huts can be rented for camping overnight.

OTHER NOTABLE RED SEA BEACHES

ABU DABBAB BEACH, MARSA ALAM, EGYPT: **Abu Dabbab is a marine preserve in the planned tourist town of Marsa Alam, built by Kuwaiti investors in 1995. Turtle, dugong, dolphin, and whale shark sightings are common here. The beach town is also the gateway to the massive Wadi el Gemal National Park and Hamata Islands.**

DAHLAK ARCHIPELAGO, ERITREA: **Off the coast of the port city of Massawa, many of the Dahlak Archipelago's 120-plus islands were part of a historic pearl fishery. Only four of the islands have permanent residents, with a total population of only about 2,500 people, all of whom speak Dahalik and maintain a traditional way of life that includes fishing and herding goats and camels. The islands have pristine beaches, a seabed littered with shipwrecks, and spectacular underwater life that, because of Eritrea's long history of conflict, has been seen by few visitors.**

UMLUJ BEACH, TABŪK, SAUDI ARABIA: **Being promoted by the Saudi government as the "Maldives of Saudi Arabia," the coast and offshore islands at Umluj are distinctive for more than 300 species of coral—four times as many as are found in the Caribbean—and unusually clear water.**

PRÍNCIPE ISLAND, SÃO TOMÉ AND PRÍNCIPE

PRAIA MARGARIDA

An African Eden where sea turtles and kingfishers outnumber people

CATEGORY: Wildlife   BEST TIME TO GO: May through October
WHAT YOU'LL EXPERIENCE: Rainforest, migrating humpback whales, few people, Gulf of Guinea

Some 130 miles (209 km) off the coast of West Africa lies the tiny, two-island nation of São Tomé and Príncipe, which is sometimes referred to as "the Galápagos of Africa." Its most admired beach is Praia Margarida. Tucked inside a verdant UNESCO Biosphere Reserve that encompasses all of Príncipe and an extensive marine area, the beach's soft blond sand can only be reached by a footpath through the rainforest or by boat on the emerald green waters surrounding the island.

Those lucky enough to visit may spot kingfishers perching in the palm trees, sea turtles in the shallows, and humpback whales in the distance (particularly during their migration from May through October). And while the occasional fishers or island residents may turn up, visitors to this beach are more likely to have the whole place to themselves.

Travelers are almost always guests of the nearby Sundy Praia, a boutique lodge in the rainforest with 16 tented villas about a 15-minute walk from the beach. The hotel arranges picnic lunches on the sand and snorkeling adventures along teeming reefs. Landlubbing guests walk over and simply relax in the shade beneath almond trees fringing the shoreline. The rest of São Tomé and Príncipe is also worth exploring, including the stunning Praia Banana, a public beach accessible through the Belo Monte Hotel. It takes a couple of days to get there from just about anywhere, so consider staying awhile.

The blue-breasted kingfisher can be found across equatorial Africa, including on Príncipe Island. It has been featured on stamps from São Tomé and Príncipe.

BOFA BEACH

A quiet East African beach town with a bohemian vibe and a nearby nature reserve

CATEGORY: Culture   **BEST TIME TO GO:** July or August
WHAT YOU'LL EXPERIENCE: Swahili ruins, kiteboarding, savanna elephants, Indian Ocean

An hour north of Mombasa, Kilifi is an ancient Swahili settlement at the mouth of a lagoon. Traditional African dhow boats can still be seen along the water's edge, while bohemian-minded remote workers take up residence at local cafés. They have discovered that Kenya's beaches—at about the same latitude as Bali and the Maldives—are among the most beautiful in the world, while comparatively untouristed and inexpensive to visit.

The beachside town of Kilifi remains largely overlooked in comparison to better-known Kenyan beaches like Diani and Watamu. However, it is becoming increasingly popular as an eco-friendly resort community along one of the Indian Ocean's most striking stretches of sand.

Bofa Beach, just north of the entrance to the lagoon known as Kilifi Creek, is a three-mile-long (5 km) swath of fine, powdery white sand backed by red-orange flowering royal poinciana and white-flowering moringa. Often nearly deserted, the Indian Ocean here is temperate and refreshing on a hot day, perfect for swimming and snorkeling, while the beach is said to rival Diani for the whitest and softest sand in Kenya.

Kilifi is a relaxed little town. Beyond the beach, the town is home to the bluff-top Mnarani National Monument and archaeological site and the remains of two 15th-century mosques that make it an ideal base for exploring.

Double-outrigger canoes called *ngalawa* line the shores of Kilifi Creek. They have been used for fishing for centuries.

WATAMU BEACH

A white-sand, snorkeling, and diving mecca on Kenya's eastern shoreline

CATEGORY: Wildlife   **BEST TIME TO GO:** July through October
WHAT YOU'LL EXPERIENCE: Tropical reefs, tide pools, Watamu Marine National Park & Reserve, Indian Ocean

Welcome to the coastal village of Watamu, where bone-white sand and swaying coconut palms meet blue-green water and fringing coral reefs. Wedged between a tidal creek and a barrier reef within the Indian Ocean, the beach's dynamic location lends itself to all kinds of activities. Snorkeling and diving are the most popular, with regular boat trips to the nearby Watamu Marine National Park & Reserve for its myriad undersea life and more than 100 species of birds.

The marine park protects more than 500 species of fish, along with turtles, manta rays, and whale sharks. Established in 1968, the area became one of Kenya's first marine parks, and in 1979 it also became a UNESCO Biosphere Reserve. Its establishment, in part, has been a major conservation effort to safeguard more than a dozen threatened species on the International Union for Conservation of Nature's Red List. The endangered guitarfish and the vulnerable brown-marbled grouper, for example, are both found here.

Undersea exploration is highly recommended, but beachgoers can also enjoy relaxing on a towel, investigating vibrant tide pools and sandbars, and venturing out on paddleboards, dugout canoes, and even kiteboards. The park is also a turtle breeding area, with green and hawksbill turtles regularly spotted, and olive ridleys, loggerheads, and leatherbacks occasionally encountered. (Give the nests and the turtles their space.)

NEARBY

Watamu is a great base for exploring nearby Gede Ruins historical monument (the remains of an ancient Swahili town dating back to the 12th century) and also the Arabuko Sokoke Forest Reserve, one of the largest stretches of forested shoreline in Africa. The forest is home to elephants, civets, vervet monkeys, baboons, and several rare bird species.

The tide and the white sand of Watamu reflect the setting sun.

LOANGO NATIONAL PARK

A wildlife paradise where the rainforest bumps up against the ocean

CATEGORY: Wildlife   **BEST TIME TO GO:** June through August
WHAT YOU'LL EXPERIENCE: Surfing hippos, forest buffalo, humpback whales, Atlantic Ocean

If someone told you there was a place where hippos dash out of the forest and into the sea, then surf the waves, would you believe it? Scenes like this happen with enough regularity in Gabon's Loango National Park that it's made the region famous. In 2004, *National Geographic* magazine even dubbed it "the land of the surfing hippos." They are said to bodysurf from one beach to another, apparently in search of food.

A trip to this remote 380,000-acre (153,780 ha) wilderness on Africa's far western shoreline can also include beach sightings of forest elephants, forest buffalo, lowland gorillas, red river hogs, chimpanzees, and even leopards. In addition, the colossal park is home to 335 bird species. And, depending on when you visit, there are also myriad sea creatures, such as humpback and killer whales, some of which can be seen from the shore.

From November through March, the beach swells with nesting olive ridley and leatherback sea turtles and hatchlings, and from July through September, migrating humpback whales arrive for breeding season. From November through April, sport fishing becomes a draw, but at no time of year does anyone ever go swimming. Remember the hippos? They're dangerous, as are the resident crocodiles.

Most guests fly to the park from Leon Mba International Airport in Gabon's capital, Libreville, and then take a 3.5-hour car or boat ride to the coast. Cruise

OPPOSITE: **A man cooks on a seaside fire on Loango Beach. Fresh fish is a staple of Gabon's cuisine.**

PAGES 266–267: **Forest elephants have been known to swim and frolic in the ocean of Loango.**

passengers aboard the *Swan Hellenic* line make a stop at the park, but most guests stay in safari camps and jungle lodges. Although the lodgings are quite comfortable, it's important to remember that this is an emerging ecotravel destination, and hiccups with transportation and other logistics aren't uncommon. In addition, tropical rains can crash the party, and there's no guarantee you'll see every animal on your list.

Loango National Park and 12 other national parks in Gabon were all established in 2002 by presidential decree to protect the nation's nature and wildlife. This was a big step for this former French colony that once relied on oil extraction and deforestation. Since the parks were established, many species have thrived, including 700 types of birds and the world's largest populations of western lowland gorillas and leatherback turtles.

OTHER SAFARI-LIKE BEACHES

CHOBE NATIONAL PARK, BOTSWANA: From May through October, elephants congregate along the Chobe River, which forms the northern boundary of the park. Visitors also spot impalas, warthogs, forest buffalo, and zebras from the sandy shore or on river cruises.

K'GARI (FORMERLY FRASER ISLAND), QUEENSLAND, AUSTRALIA: Off the coast of Queensland, K'gari is famous for its dingoes. These wild relatives of wolves and dogs are frequently spotted on beaches scavenging for food. Be careful: Sometimes they bite people.

YALA NATIONAL PARK, SRI LANKA: On the Sri Lankan coastline, this national park's shoreline is regularly visited by wild animals, including elephants, leopards, monkeys, and crocodiles. Keep your distance.

PLAGE D'ESSAOUIRA

Where bohemian counterculture meets an ancient port

CATEGORY: Sport-centric   **BEST TIME TO GO: September or October; April through June are best for wind sports**

WHAT YOU'LL EXPERIENCE: Kiteboarding, camels, ancient medina, prevailing trade winds, Atlantic Ocean

On Morocco's north Atlantic coast, Africa's "Windy City" of Essaouira is a historic port enclosed by 18th-century cannon-lined ramparts with a 1.2-mile-long (2 km) town beach on its south side. With its multicultural medina (historic district) as a backdrop and a wide corniche often lined with vendors selling juice and refreshing snacks, the city and its eponymous beach—Plage d'Essaouira—has a bohemian bent.

Essaouira dates to the fifth or sixth centuries B.C., when it first became an important transit point and port. But its breezy coastal counterculture is rooted in the 1960s, when backpackers, hippies, and artists—Jimi Hendrix famously among them—began finding their way here.

In recent years, this charismatic city has taken on another identity as an international destination for water sports, from surfing to kiteboarding. The steady and remarkably strong (especially in July and August) trade winds fuel the area's wind sports, and its long, sandy beach means that there are more protected areas closest to the medina that are best for beginners, as well as places farther south for experienced riders. These same conditions are responsible for riptides and waves, which cause some areas of the beach to be dangerous for swimming. But its wide swath of sand and promenade make it the city's most strollable waterfront. Nearby, camels sit majestically, awaiting riders to tour the nearby sand dunes.

Essaouira's northeasterly trade winds make it a great spot for kitesurfing.

CAPE MACLEAR

A sandy, swimmable, freshwater beach teeming with tropical fish

CATEGORY: Lake, river, and waterway   **BEST TIME TO GO:** April through October
WHAT YOU'LL EXPERIENCE: Cichlids, endangered species, granite outcroppings, Lake Malawi

Cape Maclear sits on the third largest body of water in Africa, a lake that spans three countries and goes by three names: Lake Nyasa in Tanzania, Lago Niassa in Mozambique, and Lake Malawi in the landlocked country of Malawi, which contains much of the lake's shoreline. One of the deepest lakes in the world, Lake Malawi is among the relatively few freshwater lakes in the region where swimming and snorkeling are possible. Elsewhere, wildlife, such as crocodiles, hippos, and even electric catfish, keep people out of the water.

Created in 1984 as the world's first freshwater national park, Lake Malawi National Park—a UNESCO World Heritage site—protects species on the Nankumba Peninsula that are endangered by poaching, including antelope and baboons. Underwater, the park is thought to have as many as 1,000 species of fish, more than any other lake in the world, with new species still being discovered.

Near the fishing village of Chembe, the gateway to the park's beaches, Cape Maclear has a shore of golden sand bordered by green grass, dense forest, and rocky granite outcroppings. Kayaking, paddleboarding, and snorkeling are popular. Otter Point is a well-known dive site for seeing the hundreds of species of cichlids, tropical freshwater fish that are remarkable for their brilliant colors and diversity.

There are 600 to 700 species of cichlids living in Lake Malawi, and more are being discovered all the time.

LANDLOCKED BEACHES

Explore unusual spots where land doesn't just meet water but surrounds it entirely.

Most of us likely picture a beach as a ribbon of sand along a seashore with crashing, or gently lapping, waves. But beaches can be found almost anywhere that water meets land. Deep in the flame-hued gorge of the Grand Canyon, for example, there's Boat Beach—a curve of red sand where the blue-green waters of Bright Angel Creek empty into the muddy Colorado River. A place of significance for the Pueblo people for millennia, the beach took on a new role in the 20th century when it became the drop-off point for tourist boats delivering guests to Phantom Ranch, a historic wilderness lodge built in 1922 in an oasis of cottonwood trees. The lodge, now part of Grand Canyon National Park, is still operational (though you have to enter a lottery to get a reservation to overnight there), and the beach remains a popular pull-out for rafters navigating the river's rapids and hikers exploring the canyon by foot. Its location—between two of Grand Canyon's only footbridges for hundreds of miles—makes it an enduring refuge for hikers and boaters.

Even more unusual, perhaps, is Playa de Gulpiyuri in Asturias, Spain. Dubbed the "smallest beach in the world" by its fans, Gulpiyuri is on neither a river nor a lake. Instead, it's a sinkhole 330 feet (100 m) from the rocky headlands of the Cantabrian Sea coast. Once one of many sea caves along the coastline, Gulpiyuri was formed when the cave's ceiling collapsed.

Rafters on the Colorado River in the Grand Canyon often stop at Boat Beach.

Ocean water from the Bay of Biscay continued to flow beneath the toppled rock, creating a golden-sand beach that only appears at low tide and is now a natural monument.

NOTABLE LANDLOCKED BEACHES

A LAKE MCKENZIE, QUEENSLAND, AUSTRALIA: On K'gari (formerly Fraser Island), this lake is fed only by rainwater—not streams or groundwater—and is ringed by fine silica sand that filters the lake's exceptionally clear water.

B JELLYFISH LAKE, ROCK ISLANDS, PALAU: Cut off from any predators and with no need to defend themselves, the golden jellyfish in this inland, saltwater lake have evolved not to sting. Snorkelers can swim with up to five million frilly jellyfish, which follow the path of the sun across the lake.

C LONE ROCK BEACH, LAKE POWELL, UTAH, U.S.A.: A beach within Glen Canyon National Recreation Area, Lone Rock offers primitive camping sites at the foot of an imposing sandstone boulder on the shores of massive, tentacled Lake Powell.

D LAGOA DO FOGO, SÃO MIGUEL, AZORES, PORTUGAL: Located in the caldera of the Água de Pau Massif volcano, which last erupted in 1652, the beach is on the shore of the highest of three crater lakes on the island of São Miguel.

E PLAYA DE GULPIYURI, ASTURIAS, SPAIN: Some say this flooded sinkhole has the smallest beach in the world.

NAMIBIA

SKELETON COAST

A spooky stretch of south African coastline known as "the end of the Earth"

CATEGORY: Remote   **BEST TIME TO GO:** May through November
WHAT YOU'LL EXPERIENCE: Shipwrecks, Skeleton Coast National Park, deserted sand dunes, surfing, Atlantic Ocean

Considered one of the least hospitable coastlines on the planet, Namibia's Skeleton Coast—300 miles (500 km) of virtually uninhabited desert between the Angola border and the old German colonial outpost of Swakopmund—isn't for everyone. But for lovers of wild, untamed beaches where one can travel for hundreds of miles and have dunes and bluffs, rocky outcroppings, and churning surf virtually to oneself, this desolate stretch of African coastline is a place of extraordinary beauty.

The coast's name refers to both the whale bones that accumulated along the beaches and the carcasses of ships, which are dashed ashore here in unusually high numbers due to the thick fog and tumultuous coastal waters. The result of the Benguela Current, this dense layer of ocean fog abutting the desert is called *cassimbo* by the locals.

This most unusual place on the planet, so rugged and brutal, is also a national park, home to lions, leopards, hyenas, and cheetahs. Offshore, there are 11 species of sharks, which feed on the large populations of fur seals, and a remarkable diversity of undersea life. Whales are also making a comeback, after nearly being hunted to extinction in the area. The sand dunes here rise hundreds of feet, making much of the coastline only accessible via a light plane air safari or off-road vehicles with guides. It's not an easy place to experience, nor one to go for a casual swim, but it's a deeply memorable one.

HISTORY

The coast's name comes from author John Henry Marsh, who coined the name in the title of his 1944 book documenting one of the prominent shipwrecks off this infamously dangerous stretch of the Atlantic Ocean—the 1942 wreck of the Blue Star Line *Dunedin Star*.

Hundreds of shipwrecks, along with the bones of whales and seals, gave the Skeleton Coast its grim name.

KISAWA SANCTUARY BEACH

Swim with dugongs on a subtropical island inside a national park.

CATEGORY: Wildlife   **BEST TIME TO GO:** July through October for humpback whales
WHAT YOU'LL EXPERIENCE: High-end ecotourism, 2,000 species of fish, reefs made by 3D printers, Indian Ocean

Benguerra is the second-largest island in the 540-square-mile (1,400 km²) Bazaruto Archipelago National Park, a nature and marine reserve created in 1971 to protect Mozambique's exceptionally biodiverse Bazaruto Archipelago. The islands are known for their spectacular underwater life, including the last viable population on the East Africa coast of manatee-like dugongs, which live in the seagrass beds that surround the beaches.

Bazaruto's five barrier islands have diverse ecosystems, from sand dunes to grasslands, mangroves to extensive coral reefs. They're so well protected and undeveloped that the local population remains small. (Plus, the islands are neither easy nor inexpensive to visit.) Only about 5,000 people live in the archipelago, most of whom work in fishing and tourism. On Benguerra, in particular, there are only a handful of accommodations, including Kisawa Sanctuary resort, parts of which were built with an environmentally sustainable mix of sand and seawater using 3D printing technology. The pristine white-sand beaches on the aquamarine waters of the cove are perfect for paddleboarding and swimming.

On the southern tip of the island, the 740-acre (300 ha) Kisawa Sanctuary opened in conjunction with the Bazaruto Center for Scientific Studies (BCSS), a conservation and research nonprofit funded by the five-star resort.

MARINE LIFE

BCSS has a five-star PADI dive center that documents the ecology of the western Indian Ocean. Visitors can help scientists take a tally of significant marine life, including scalloped hammerhead sharks, manta rays, humpback whales, dolphins, three species of sea turtles, dwarf minke whales, rare ornate eagle rays, and sailfish.

Between 150 and 250 dugongs, related to manatees, live off the coast of Kisawa. They are critically endangered in East Africa.

CHANGUU ISLAND BEACH

Take a traditional dhow to a historic prison island.

CATEGORY: Unusual   **BEST TIME TO GO:** June through October (dry season)
WHAT YOU'LL EXPERIENCE: Aldabra giant tortoises, historic prison hospital, Indian Ocean

A short boat ride from the UNESCO World Heritage site of Stone Town of Zanzibar, there's a would-be prison turned yellow fever hospital that lures visitors to its lush, forested, beach-lined shores. Today, Changuu's history has a new chapter as a sanctuary for Earth's longest-living animal, the majestic Aldabra giant tortoise.

Changuu is the Swahili word for a type of fish that's abundant in the surrounding waters. The area has been part of the Changuu-Bawe Marine Conservation Area since 2009, protecting both its underwater life and its cultural heritage, including several noteworthy shipwrecks and the island's ruins. The clear, cerulean-blue waters are home to bluefins, barracuda, electric rays, and electric eels, among other deep-water species.

Most visitors reach the island by dhow—a 30-minute trip on a traditional African sailboat—and spend the day exploring the island's historic prison, pristine sandbar beach, and the tortoise sanctuary. The massive animals can weigh up to 550 pounds (250 kg) and live twice as long as humans—some are believed to be more than 200 years old. The tortoises are native to the Indian Ocean atoll of Aldabra, in Seychelles. In 1919, the Seychelles governor sent four of the majestic tortoises to Zanzibar as a gift. The Changuu colony includes those original animals and their descendants, and today totals between 100 and 200 tortoises.

HISTORY

In the 1860s, the first sultan of Zanzibar gave the island to two Arab slave traders. When the British took control of Tanzania in 1890, they regarded Changuu Island as just isolated enough to warehouse criminals. But the prison island was instead used to quarantine new arrivals to Zanzibar during epidemics well into the early 1900s.

Boats are the only way to get to Changuu Island.

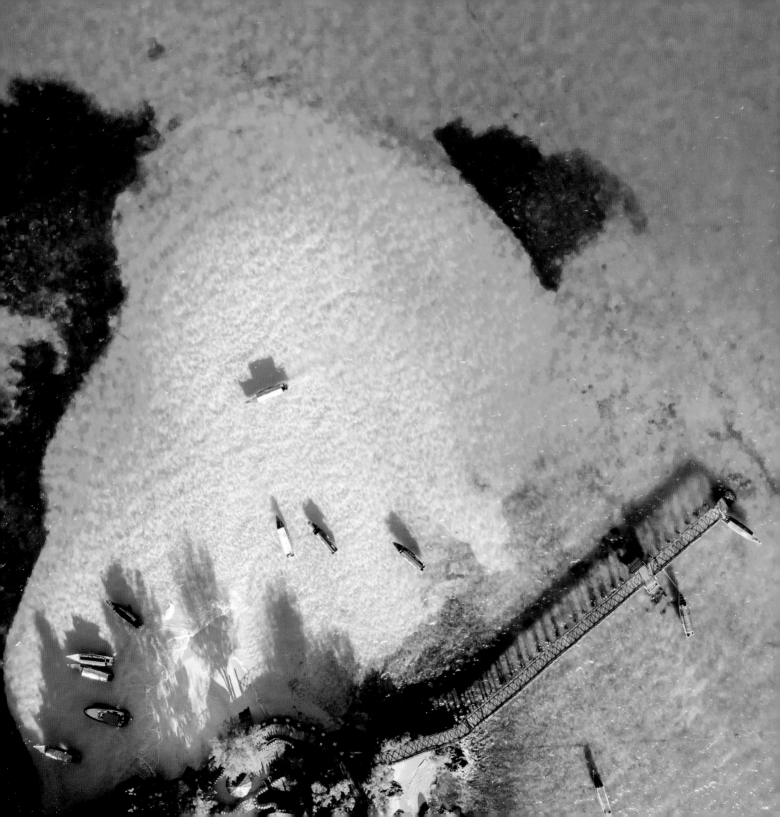

BUTIAMA BEACH

A Swahili coast island paradise where visitors can swim with whale sharks

---

CATEGORY: Wildlife   **BEST TIME TO GO: October through March**
WHAT YOU'LL EXPERIENCE: Coral reefs, Mafia Island Marine Park, Indian Ocean

If you've ever dreamed of escaping to a little-visited island to see the world's largest fish, Butiama Beach is calling. This stretch of sand lies along the western shore of the largest island of the Mafia Archipelago, just off the coast of mainland Tanzania. Visitors who make the journey to this little-explored island spend their days lazing around in the sand, hanging out in laid-back villages, and snorkeling with majestic, 39-foot (12 m) whale sharks. These gentle giants return to the island every summer to eat up the resident plankton. During guided boat trips, visitors can snorkel beside whale sharks while following strict guidelines, which prohibit getting close or touching the fish. Thanks to a healthy reef system protected within the Mafia Island Marine Park since 1995, the scuba diving is also pretty spectacular.

If you're already in Tanzania, getting to Butiama isn't all that difficult. Short 30-minute charter flights arrive regularly from Dar es Salaam and Zanzibar Island, and there are also connections between most of the popular safari destinations. Still, only around 7,000 people visit Mafia Island each year. As a result, both the chilled-out vibe and the local culture have endured. Trips to the marine park, whale sharks, and nearby islands can be arranged through Butiama Beach Lodge. The accommodation is right by the sea, and it's possible to walk for miles along the fine blond sand without encountering another soul.

The plankton-eating whale shark, seen here off the coast of Butiama, is the largest fish alive today. The biggest whale shark ever accurately measured was 61.7 feet (18.8 m) long.

CAMPS BAY BEACH

A swanky urban beach for nightlife lovers and jet-setters

CATEGORY: Iconic **BEST TIME TO GO:** December or January
WHAT YOU'LL EXPERIENCE: Tide pool, Rotunda, the Twelve Apostles, Atlantic Ocean

I n the affluent Cape Town suburb of Camps Bay, Camps Bay Beach is a buzzy urban beach lined by a promenade of trendy bars and upscale restaurants, with a reputation that precedes it. The beach's fine sand and photogenic setting—with Table Mountain and the Twelve Apostles mountain range as a dramatic backdrop—have made it South Africa's see-and-be-seen party spot for both well-heeled Capetonians and the international jet set.

Until 1887, Camps Bay was largely undeveloped. Then, Victoria Road was completed using convict labor and named in honor of the Queen's 1888 Jubilee. The new road enabled Capetonians to bicycle from the city to the beach, and was soon followed by a tramway, human-made tide pools, and the beach's iconic structure, the geometrical-domed Victorian Rotunda, a once-glamorous turn-of-the-century event venue and pavilion which is now part of The Bay Hotel Cape Town.

With chilly seawater temperatures year-round, the ocean here is better seen than swam. But that doesn't keep Camps Bay from being swarmed by beachgoers—including a large contingent of Europeans—during the Southern Hemisphere summer high season. For a somewhat less-chilly swim, Camps Bay's tide pool of walled-off seawater tends to be a bit warmer than the ocean alongside it.

The cool winter is a less-busy, less-windy time to visit Camps Bay, and you are more likely to see whales.

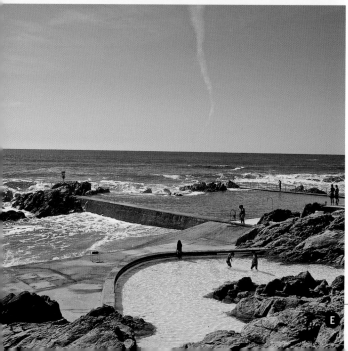

OTHER NOTABLE OCEAN POOLS

A CARPA OLIVERA, MAZATLÁN, MEXICO: Built in 1914 when ocean pools were the rage across Europe, this seaside pool on Olas Altas Beach off Mazatlán's historic *malecón*, or boardwalk, is unusual for its sculptural concrete slide. Having fallen into disrepair, the pool was restored in 2015.

B BRONTE BATHS, SYDNEY, AUSTRALIA: Sydney's seashore has more than 30 open-air ocean pools. Public and accessible to anyone, these egalitarian swim places are sometimes carved into cliffs and rocks, sans beach, but Bronte has a pretty little sandy bay alongside it.

C KASTRUP SØBAD, COPENHAGEN, DENMARK: A newer sea bath, Kastrup was built in 2005 at the end of a boardwalk on Øresund sound. Referred to as a lake rather than a pool because of its size, this snail-shaped swim hole sits just south of Amager Strandpark, with views of Saltholm Island and Sweden.

D BUDE SEA POOL, CORNWALL, ENGLAND, UNITED KINGDOM: At the southern tip of the United Kingdom, Cornwall has some of the country's best weather. Built in 1930 at Summerleaze Beach, the Bude Sea Pool is a sheltered swim spot for families and a hangout for surfers.

E PISCINA DAS MARÉS, PORTO, PORTUGAL: Leça da Palmeira beach's saltwater pools were designed by famed Portuguese architect Álvaro Siza Vieira. Built between 1961 and 1966, the two pools—one for adults and another for kids—are known among architecture enthusiasts for how well integrated they are into the coastal landscape.

PATERNOSTER BEACH

A historic fishing village known for its beach and its fresh seafood

---

CATEGORY: Historical   **BEST TIME TO GO:** March through September
WHAT YOU'LL EXPERIENCE: Cape Columbine Nature Reserve, wildflowers, Atlantic Ocean

One of the oldest fishing villages in South Africa, Paternoster, on the country's rugged west coast, has close ties to the sea— from its thriving lobster and deep-sea fisheries to mussel harvesting and, more recently, its kabeljou, oyster, and abalone farms. Paternoster's beach is lined with whitewashed limestone cottages with Mediterranean-blue accents, and its historic hotel (a circa 1863 building) is a kitschy landmark known for its Panty Bar, where the ceiling is adorned with donated women's underwear.

South Africa's beaches are famous for being both beautiful and a bit chilly, despite the region's mild climate, and the water temperature here rarely reaches 70°F (21°C). That doesn't stop the beach from being a destination for everything from kitesurfing (thanks to the coast's consistent breeze) to kayaking. But swimming is best done in the hotel pool, as the seawater is quite cold. Dramatic swaths of year-round wildflowers are another draw, as is the nearby Cape Columbine Nature Reserve, which has the last manually controlled lighthouse to be built in South Africa (commissioned in 1936).

Despite Paternoster's tiny population of 2,000, its abundance of fresh fish and excellent South African wine has helped put its seaside restaurants and wine bars on the map. One local delicacy, *bokkoms,* or fish biltong (salted and dried mullet), can be seen air-drying along the beachfront.

Clouds roll in over the pristine beach and fishing village of Paternoster.

NOTABLE BEACH SNACKS

A STICKY RICE WITH MANGO, THAILAND AND MUCH OF SOUTHEAST ASIA: There's often crossover between street food and beach food. In Southeast Asia, that means night market staples like mango and sticky rice are a seaside favorite.

B FISH BILTONG, PATERNOSTER, SOUTH AFRICA: Also known as *bokkoms,* these salted and dried whole mullets are a delicacy along the west coast of South Africa.

C BLUE CRABS, MARYLAND AND THE MID-ATLANTIC, U.S.A.: In the Chesapeake Bay area, there's nothing more iconic than a bucket of steamed blue crabs coated in Old Bay seasoning and served on butcher paper–covered tables overlooking the water.

D BACALAÍTOS, PIÑONES, PUERTO RICO: Salt cod fritters are popular throughout much of the Caribbean, Brazil, and Portugal. But this flat, puffy Puerto Rican version, sold at the kiosks that line the beaches in Piñones, is made with the island's characteristic ingredients, including sazón, sofrito, cilantro, olives, capers, and white rum.

E SCALLOPS IN KARI GOSSE, SAINT-GILDAS-DE-RHUYS, FRANCE: From April through September, beach restaurants in Brittany serve scallops in the shell, seasoned with kari gosse, a Breton spice blend of clove, ginger, turmeric, chili, cinnamon, and pepper.

F YANIQUEQUES OR YANIKEKE, BOCA CHICA, DOMINICAN REPUBLIC: Though it takes its name from the johnnycake, an American standby, this uniquely Dominican beach staple is fried, not griddle-cooked. These thin, crispy discs of crackling dough sprinkled with salt are most associated with one popular beach, Boca Chica.

G BHELPURI, MUMBAI, INDIA: This dish, made with puffed rice, boiled potatoes, chutneys, and spices, is often sold by vendors wheeling carts along the sand, and is served in paper cones.

LA DIGUE, SEYCHELLES

ANSE SOURCE D'ARGENT

A pink-sand beauty that's tough to reach and tougher to leave

CATEGORY: **Remote**   BEST TIME TO GO: **May through September**
WHAT YOU'LL EXPERIENCE: **Granite boulders, coral reef, giant tortoises, Indian Ocean**

Does Anse Source d'Argent look familiar? It should. This remote and delightful cove on La Digue, one of 115 islands that make up Seychelles, is one of the most photographed beaches on Earth—and for good reason. Defined by its clear blue-green water, rosy sand, and fantastic boulders, this is surely one of the world's most beautiful beaches, and it features prominently in advertising campaigns that strive to invoke paradise.

Like any postcard-pretty beach that manages to remain relatively pristine, Anse Source d'Argent is tough to reach. Most visitors come from the main island, Mahé, then take a two-hour ferry ride across the Indian Ocean to La Digue. From there, it's a bike ride or a walk to L'Union Estate, an old vanilla and coconut plantation where the owners collect a fee (around U.S. $17) in exchange for a day pass to access the beach. The former estate now features a giant tortoise enclosure and a small museum, both of which are worth a look before continuing on a half-mile (0.8 km), palm-fringed pathway to the world-famous shore.

Once you've arrived, snap your own ridiculously stunning photos and relax on the light pink sand beneath swaying coconut palms, with some fresh coconut water or fruit juice in hand (local vendors at makeshift beach shacks are happy to add rum, too). Eventually, you'll want to frolic among the

OPPOSITE: The waters off Anse Source d'Argent are warm, clear, and range from turquoise to blue.

PAGES 294–295: The rock formations of Anse Source d'Argent have been smoothed over time and look sculptural.

> *"Walking barefoot into an aquamarine ocean, touching its ivory powder sand beaches, or exploring wildlife by bicycle is easy on La Digue."*
>
> —NATALIE LEFEVRE, *EURONEWS*

smooth granite boulders and wade into the shallow, clear water. Thanks to a nearby fringe reef, the water is calm and the snorkeling is top-notch (you'll likely see butterfly fish, parrotfish, and triggerfish). And for those who don't like getting their hair wet, locals rent translucent kayaks to paddle over the reef, where sea turtles are regularly spotted.

Despite the difficulty in getting here, the beach does tend to get crowded around midday. Avoid this by showing up early in the morning or late in the afternoon. Sunsets are spectacular and most everyone has cleared out by then, so consider staying overnight on the island. There are numerous hotels, cabins, and traditional island accommodations to choose from.

PART FIVE

ASIA

A bird's-eye view of the limestone cliffs and beaches of the Railay Peninsula near Krabi, Thailand (page 344)

KELEBEKLER VADISI BEACH

This undeveloped beach is worth the hike or boat trip to get there.

CATEGORY: Wildlife   **BEST TIME TO GO:** June through September
WHAT YOU'LL EXPERIENCE: Butterflies, Babadağ mountain, *gulet* boats, Aegean Sea

South of the busy resort town of Ölüdeniz on Turkey's Muğla coast (the so-called Turkish Riviera), there's a cove whose inaccessibility has been its greatest strength. Only reachable by sea, or via a grueling full-day hike along a portion of the Lycian Way trail, Kelebekler Vadisi (Butterfly Valley) Beach has been spared the package holiday hordes that descend on the once pristine, now Instagram-famous Blue Lagoon and its adjoining beach. This makes it unique in a region overcome by tourism development.

At the base of 6,460-foot-tall (1,969 m) Babadağ, Kelebekler Vadisi takes its name from the 100 or so varieties of butterflies that populate this long, narrow valley planted with peaches, grapes, pomegranates, and citrus. The deep, narrow crease in the coastal Taurus Mountains extends inland for nearly two miles (3.2 km), with cliffs that reach as high as 1,310 feet (400 m). It straddles the Lycian Way trail, which winds along 320 miles (515 km) of Turkey's Mediterranean coast and takes 30 to 45 days to complete. Among the winged species that call this place home is the famous black, orange, and white Jersey tiger butterfly, which is typically spotted in early June.

The valley has been protected by the Turkish government from any permanent construction since 1995 as a First Degree Natural Protected Area. Most visitors arrive at the beach by sea. Some come with tours in a *gulet*

A woman strolls the white-sand beach of Kelebekler Vadisi.

ABOVE: **Boat tours to Kelebekler Vadisi typically depart from nearby Ölüdeniz.**

OPPOSITE: **More than 100 butterfly species have been spotted in the valley, including the Jersey Tiger.**

boat, a traditional two- or three-mast schooner-style sailboat, while others arrive by ferry or yacht. Since development is banned at the fairy tale–like white-sand beach, there are only temporary structures, tipis, and tents for accommodations, one small restaurant, and basic bathroom services. This is a place for quiet communion with nature—swimming, sunbathing, and wandering the valley floor to experience its fluttering namesakes. For more adventurous visitors, there's cliff jumping, paragliding, and rock climbing.

KELEBEKLER VADISI BEACH **301**

IZTUZU PLAJI

Saved from development to protect endangered turtles, this beach is a knockout.

CATEGORY: **Wildlife**   BEST TIME TO GO: **July through August**
WHAT YOU'LL EXPERIENCE: **Dalyan River, loggerhead and green sea turtles, Köyceğiz Lake, Mediterranean Sea**

This captivating 2.8-mile (4.5 km) yellow-sand beach sits in the southern Turkish province of Muğla, where the tangled Dalyan River connects Köyceğiz Lake and the Mediterranean Sea. Considered by many to be among the most beautiful beaches in Turkey, Iztuzu Plaji is celebrated globally for its role in preserving endangered sea turtles.

The Köyceğiz-Dalyan Special Environmental Protection Area, which includes Iztuzu, was the life's work of June Haimoff, a wealthy British expat turned artist and conservationist who settled there in the 1980s. Both loggerhead and green sea turtles have historically laid their eggs along the beach's undeveloped shores, between Radar Hill and Delik Island, and protecting these endangered species became Haimoff's passion. She relentlessly advocated with the Turkish government to halt resort construction.

The beach is now a protected zone, where even the water taxis that regularly transport people have been specially configured to protect the turtle population. Most visitors come from the river town of Dalyan, just inland, by boat. Though you can make it to Iztuzu by road, the Dalyan River boats have the advantage of stopping at the region's stinky but therapeutic mud baths and visiting the Kaunos Tombs of the Kings, which were carved into the cliff faces just upriver between the fifth and second centuries B.C.

A bird's-eye view of the mountains that surround the golden sand of Iztuzu Plaji

PANTAI MERAH

Komodo dragons roam this beach where the water is turquoise and the sand is pink.

CATEGORY: Unusual   **BEST TIME TO GO:** April through June
WHAT YOU'LL EXPERIENCE: Green hills, mangrove forests, vibrant coral, Savu Sea

When people think about Indonesia's Komodo Island, they mostly think about the eponymous national park and its giant, world-famous lizards. But there's a lesser-known natural attraction that certainly holds its own: Pantai Merah, more commonly known as Pink Beach, is one of only about 12 beaches in the world with a blushing shoreline.

The unique hue of the sand comes from an accumulation of broken red coral and shells left behind by foraminifera—tiny marine creatures with red-and-pink shells. The microscopic organisms live in the coral reefs offshore, and after they die, their crushed shells wash up and mix with the beach sand.

If you scoop up a handful of sand and let it run through your fingers, you'll find both white and pink grains; that mix of colors remains consistent regardless of how deep you dig. The unusual sand color seems all the more impressive in the context of its surrounding scenery: green hills, azure skies, and turquoise water—and the occasional Komodo dragon! The world's largest living lizard, the creatures can grow more than nine feet (3 m) long and have scaly skin, serrated teeth, and potent venom. They can also run up to 12.5 miles an hour (20 kph), so visitors should maintain a respectful distance for their own safety.

Exploring the water and mangrove forests by kayak is also an option, and beneath the surface, things get interesting, too. Snorkelers can enter from

The sand looks pinkest at dawn and dusk.

> *"The rich coral reefs of Komodo host a great diversity of species, and the strong currents of the sea attract the presence of sea turtles, whales, dolphins and dugongs."*
> —UNESCO WORLD HERITAGE CONVENTION

the shore and find hard and soft corals, exotic fish, and other marine life gliding around the coral reefs. The island's diverse terrestrial and marine habitats led to Komodo National Park becoming a UNESCO World Heritage site in 1991. The entire place is a haven for travelers who appreciate pristine landscapes and unusual animal species.

Depending on what time of day you visit, the beach may not always appear as pink as social media would have you believe. In the harsh afternoon sunlight, the sand looks more white. But the pink shade brightens during the golden hours, dawn and dusk. Regardless of when you visit, the remote location and otherworldly beauty of Pantai Merah make the long journey more than worth it.

There are limited transportation options to this uninhabited island, and a visit requires advance planning. There are no restaurants, hotels, or restrooms at the beach, so you'll need to show up with the essentials, like snacks and sunscreen. Accessing the beach involves a boat ride from Labuan Bajo on the nearby island of Flores. On a slower vessel, the trip takes around three hours, though speedboats can reach the beach in about half that time. Sailing trips and cruises that stop at the beach make the journey all the more enjoyable—and are in high demand (in other words, book early). However you decide to get to Pantai Merah, having an experienced guide is ideal, especially considering the potential encounters with Komodo dragons.

The pink sand of Pantai Merah is thanks to the shells of foraminifera, single-cell marine organisms.

OTHER NOTABLE PINK BEACHES

You'll find other blushing beaches in far-flung corners of the world, from Bermuda to the Bahamas, the Philippines to Greece. Although the exact number of pink-sand beaches is up for debate, there are a few of them:

A HORSESHOE BAY, BERMUDA: Horseshoe Bay boasts pale pink sand and calm, clear waters, and is popular with swimmers, snorkelers, and sunbathers.

B PINK SANDS BEACH, HARBOUR ISLAND, BAHAMAS: Turquoise water meets pink sand on Harbour Island's eastern shoreline, where the 100-foot-wide (30 m) beach extends for three miles (4.8 km). A nearby stable rents horses for a ride on the beach.

C SPIAGGIA ROSA, BUDELLI, ITALY: Near Sardinia, this beach showcases pink sand bordered by granite rocks.

D TIKEHAU, FRENCH POLYNESIA: An oval lagoon on the island of Tikehau is rimmed with a pink-and-white-sand beach frequented by scuba divers and kayakers.

E PACHIA AMMOS, CRETE, GREECE: Pachia Ammos Beach offers gold-and-pink sand surrounded by mountains and is ideal for water sports.

F PFEIFFER BEACH, CALIFORNIA, U.S.A.: Manganese garnet runoff from nearby hillsides has resulted in this beach's pinkish-purple sand, which is best appreciated at sunset. The beach is also home to the famous Keyhole Arch rock formation.

TANJUNG AAN BEACH

On the quiet south coast of Lombok, an unusual cultural festival celebrates sea worms.

CATEGORY: Culture   **BEST TIME TO GO:** February or March through April
WHAT YOU'LL EXPERIENCE: Colorful *warungs*, Sasak culture, surfing, Pacific Ocean

On the south coast of Lombok are a series of beaches, each more idyllic than the last. In contrast to Bali, its comparably crowded sister island, Lombok remains relatively quiet and minimally visited by tourists much of the year, except for the high season months of June through August. This is surprising, as Lombok has a gorgeous coastline of warm turquoise water, excellent surf, white-sand beaches, and the car-free Gili Islands just offshore.

Each February or March, in accordance with the traditional lunar calendar, Lombok celebrates Bau Nyale, a festival with a name that literally means "catching sea worms." It's a major cultural event for the local Sasak people, and thousands wade into the ocean, gathering the glistening green, brown, and yellow sea worms (a type of palolo worm that thrives in the warm South Pacific waters) known as *nyale*. The nyale are then steamed or barbecued and eaten as a delicacy and an aphrodisiac.

The Sasak people of Lombok are related to the Balinese, but most are Muslim, not Hindu, and have distinct cultural traditions, including Bau Nyale. Historically, the event was held at nearby Seger Beach. But the Indonesian government's recent efforts to expand the perceived success of Bali's tourism economy with a plan called "five new Balis" has brought a development push to the region. This includes the construction of a racetrack at Seger Beach

OPPOSITE: Picturesque Tanjung Aan Beach is set in a cove between the hills.

PAGES 312–313: Local fishing boats ply the crystal clear waters off Tanjung Aan Beach.

and the relocation of the festival to Tanjung Aan, a 1.25-mile (2 km) stretch of white sand.

But the festival's essence has remained the same. It honors a princess, Mandalika, from the ancient Tonjang Beru kingdom. According to legend, the princess was so beautiful and widely desired that fights and rivalries broke out for her affection. Not wanting to see harm come to anyone on her behalf, Mandalika is said to have sacrificed herself to the sea, where she became a nyale.

Along with catching and eating sea worms, the festival also includes performances, such as *gendang beleq*, a traditional Sasak style of dance and drumming, and *peresean*, a martial art competition using sticks and shields. There's also a parade of dance, costumes, and songs that culminates with the ceremonial crowning of the princess.

While the sea worm festival and its deep cultural and historical significance is one reason to seek out Tanjung Aan Beach—just 45 minutes from Lombok's international airport—the shoreline is worth a visit any time of year. From the Bukit Merese (Merese Hill) viewpoint, a 10-minute walk from the beach, you get a wide view of the bay and nearby islands, while other parts have *warungs* (small, family-run shops, mostly eateries) and beach shacks.

VAADHOO ISLAND GLOWING BEACH

A white-sand bay on an Indian Ocean atoll with extraordinary bioluminescence

CATEGORY: Nature **BEST TIME TO GO:** June through October
WHAT YOU'LL EXPERIENCE: Tiny crustaceans, crystal clear water, Indian Ocean

A "Sea of Stars" is what locals call this occasionally bioluminescent beach on Vaadhoo Island—one of the 26 coral atolls dotting the Indian Ocean that comprise the Maldives. The legendary phenomenon takes place on dark summer nights and is most pronounced about five days after a full moon.

Although people originally thought the blue glow was coming from phytoplankton, which shine momentarily when they're disturbed in the water, scientists recently found otherwise. On Vaadhoo, the glorious but sporadic displays come from ostracod crustaceans, also known as seed shrimp, which secrete a bioluminescent mucus as a defense mechanism and during courtship. The shrimp are about a millimeter long, and their glow on the beach, which lasts several seconds, is thought to be the result of a mass mortality event (scientists are unsure of the cause). Maldivians refer to these events as Redhan lun, and revere them in folktales.

While it may be difficult to plan a trip that coincides with this particular display, it's worth trying. Other draws to Vaadhoo include stone prayer mounds and an ornate 17th-century mosque. The small island (population around 500) is within the Raa Atoll, located about 85 miles (136 km) from Velana International Airport. You can get to Raa in a seaplane, on a domestic flight, or in a boat, which takes about four hours.

The beach glows with blue light emitted from the mass mortality of seed shrimp.

ALL ABOUT BIOLUMINESCENCE

A host of creatures light up beaches around the world with fascinating, if fleeting, displays.

I f it's bioluminescence you're after, there are plenty of beaches around the world where phytoplankton (and other creatures, too) provide a predictably sparkly experience. This phenomenon is carried out by a variety of organisms, both on land and in the sea, including bacteria, plankton, fireflies, worms, snails, fish, jellyfish, and even sharks.

Mesmerizing displays of bioluminescent creatures can be observed in forests illuminated by fireflies, caves adorned with glowworms, and secluded island shores dotted with plankton. Bioluminescent creatures either produce the compound called luciferin, which emits light, or they consume organisms that do. Some bioluminescent animals light up when stressed. Others use their light to attract mates, blend into their surroundings, lure prey, communicate with allies, or confuse enemies.

Some adventurers plan trips around specific events, like the sparkling, mating fireworms that swim to the surface in Bermuda on the third night after a full moon in summer and fall, or the emergence of bright-blue firefly squid in Japan every April and May. One of the top spots to experience these dazzling creatures is Puerto Rico's Bioluminescent Bay, which has the brightest-glowing dinoflagellates (marine plankton) in the world, according to Guinness World Records. Other popular bioluminescent beaches include New Zealand's Matakatia Bay and the shores of Koh Rong Island in Cambodia.

Dinoflagellate algae light up the water in Tasmania beneath the Milky Way.

YALONG WAN

Where China's hurried growth meets the country's most tropical island

CATEGORY: Iconic   **BEST TIME TO GO: Year-round**
WHAT YOU'LL EXPERIENCE: Mangrove forests, human-made archipelago, South China Sea

In the past few decades, Sanya, on the south coast of the island of Hainan in the South China Sea, has grown from a small town to a high-rise city of more than a million people. It is now Hainan's second-largest city. The island, a bit smaller than Taiwan, can be reached from the mainland by a ferry across the 12-mile-wide (19 km) Qiongzhou Strait. It's increasingly popular with international tourists, who have descended on its opulent resorts to the tune of some 60 million visitors a year. Its bay is home to Phoenix Island, a human-made resort archipelago—often compared to glitzy Dubai—in what had previously been an unspoiled tropical backwater.

East of Sanya, Yalong Wan (Asian Dragon Bay) offers a glimpse of what Hainan's south coast beaches were like when they were backed by mangrove forests and dense jungle instead of high-rise condominiums and office buildings. Yalong's 4.7-mile (7.5 km) beach is sheltered and calm, which allows for swimming. It's a contrast to many nearby beaches, where entering the water is considered unsafe and prohibitions are strictly enforced.

While Yalong Wan, like Sanya, has been transformed in recent years, it remains among Hainan's most beautiful beaches. Designated as a National Resort District, it's also home to many of the island's most luxurious hotels. But compared to other tropical locales where you might find a Ritz Carlton or St. Regis, the resorts along Yalong's white sand are a bargain.

The landmark totem pole, showing images of Chinese legends, stands in the middle of Yalong Bay Central Square near the beach.

GALGIBAGA BEACH

An undeveloped beach where endangered olive ridley turtles nest

CATEGORY: **Wildlife**   BEST TIME TO GO: **April through October**
WHAT YOU'LL EXPERIENCE: **Pine forest, Portuguese colonial influences, Arabian Sea**

A Portuguese colony until 1961, Goa became the go-to bohemian beach destination for a generation of counterculture wanderers from Europe, the United States, Australia, and other countries where a free-spirited sensibility had taken hold among the young. The beaches of this small Indian state on the Arabian Sea have since had an outsize reputation.

This stretch of coast is equally well known for its all-night beach parties as it is for its seeker spirituality and wellness culture, thanks to its white sand, colorful stilted beach shacks, full moon festivities, and thriving yoga scene. But in the far south of the state, Galgibaga—also known as Turtle Beach—is quiet and uncommonly pristine.

Considered among the cleanest beaches in the country, Galgibaga distinguishes itself from Goa's more developed, party-happy beaches by embracing environmental conservation and the protection of the endangered olive ridley sea turtle. The second smallest sea turtle, it has a distinctive heart-shaped shell and olive green color. Year after year, females return to the beach to lay their eggs—typically 80 to 120 per season—for what is known as arribada, or synchronized arrival.

The shore here is free from the beach huts offering Ayurvedic massages, snacks such as Goan prawn sambar curry, and affordable accommodations

OPPOSITE: **A young olive ridley sea turtle struggles against the swell off Galgibaga.**

PAGES 322-323: **Huts and coconut palms line the golden sand of Turtle Beach.**

found elsewhere along the coast. There are only a couple of places set back from the beach to stay, and there's little to do beyond turtle-spotting and enjoying the tranquility of one of Goa's least developed beaches.

OTHER NOTABLE GOAN BEACHES

PALOLEM: Facing Canacona Island, which is known for its monkey population, Palolem Beach is a long curve lined with beach huts. It has calm water, and despite its silent discos is a bit more relaxed than some of the nearby party beaches.

AGONDA AND MORJIM: At the other two Goan beaches frequented by olive ridley turtles, Agonda (near Palolem) and Morjim in the north, the local government is making a concerted effort at conservation. Morjim, at the mouth of the Chapora River estuary, is also known for the large number of Russian immigrants who have settled there, and for water sports, including both kitesurfing and beginner surfing.

ANJUNA AND VAGATOR: Well-known stops along the so-called hippie trail of the 1950s to 1970s, when Western counterculture first descended on Goa's beaches, Anjuna and Vagator are Goa's go-to spots for clubbing, electronic dance and trance music, and the area's famous full moon parties.

MANDREM: Mandrem is among the best places on the Goan coast for water sports. January through March are the best for windsurfing and kiteboarding. In North Goa, Mandrem—and nearby Querim—are a bit less crowded than the beaches farther south.

VARKALA, INDIA

PAPANASAM BEACH

A South Indian beach where the Arabian Sea washes away your sins

CATEGORY: **Culture**   BEST TIME TO GO: **October through March**
WHAT YOU'LL EXPERIENCE: **Pink cliffs, Ayurveda treatments, Arabian Sea**

Because beaches have a leisure-time reputation, it's easy to forget that they can have deeper significance. In southern India, on the Malabar Coast of Kerala, Papanasam Beach (also known as Varkala) is revered as a sacred place—one where sins can be washed clean in the water of the Arabian Sea. For India's Hindu population, the beach here, as well as the nearby town, temple, and holy center, are among the region's most spiritually meaningful sites.

The beach itself has striking golden sand surrounded by pink laterite cliffs—the only coastal cliffs in Kerala and a national geological monument. The Indian government designated the Varkala cliff section as the country's first geopark to both protect the area and promote it as a geotourism destination. It draws both worshippers and sunbathers, as well as surfers, wellness enthusiasts, and nature lovers who recommend the gentle two-hour (5 mile/8 km) hike from Varkala to Kappil Beach, to the north, which passes largely undeveloped beaches like Odayam, and quiet fishing villages.

Varkala is also an important center for the practice of Ayurveda, the Hindu system of traditional medicine founded more than 5,000 years ago that includes everything from yoga and massage to diet and acupuncture. And, unlike Goa to the north, which is also known for attracting spiritual seekers from the West, Varkala isn't a party town.

Pink laterite cliffs stand sentinel around Papanasam Beach.

BEACHES ON THE BIG SCREEN

All over the world, sandy shores and glittering waves have starring roles in classic films.

Imagine a beach that clings to your memory like fine-grain sand on wet skin. Is it someplace you've actually been or a place you've only journeyed to on-screen? Maybe it looks like a parade of pickup trucks racing across Oregon's iconic Cannon Beach in the opening scene of 1985's *The Goonies*. Or Elvis shimmying his hips, guitar in hand, at the Coco Palms Resort in Kauai, Hawaii, in *Blue Hawaii* (1961). Or Tom Hanks unkempt and unhinged, alone on a beach with only a volleyball as a companion in 2000's *Cast Away*. Or a New England coastline crowded with families and fishers on a perfect summer day disrupted by something menacing beneath the surface, as in *Jaws* (1975), filmed on Martha's Vineyard in Massachusetts.

In pop culture, as in life, beaches play many roles. They function as everything from an escape from busy modern-day life to a place of forced isolation, à la *Lost*, the TV series, which filmed some beach scenes on the North Shore of Oahu. They represent joyous abandon and carefree innocence, as in the bubblegum surf flicks of the 1950s and '60s (1959's *Gidget* most famously, which was filmed in Malibu, California), and the frightening depths of the unknown just offshore, as in the 2016 thriller *The Shallows*, starring Blake Lively, which was filmed in New South Wales and Queensland, Australia.

But these films, in which a beach plays a starring role, are also often about various kinds of searching—communing with nature, grieving, falling in love,

Leonardo DiCaprio in *The Beach*, which was filmed on the Thai island of Ko Phi Phi Le

finding solace or human connection in a quiet, unhurried place. The beach, a borderland on the edge of land and sea, becomes someplace where opposites find each other. In the 1988 Barbara Hershey and Bette Midler classic *Beaches*, for example, a multidecade friendship begins under the boardwalk in Atlantic City (New Jersey, U.S.A.) between two girls with very different lives. Ultimately, they share a complicated story—and beaches from coast to coast.

Tom Hanks on the Fiji island of Monuriki acts in *Cast Away* with his co-star, Wilson.

The coast of South Carolina plays a similar role in *The Notebook*, the 2004 Ryan Gosling and Rachel McAdams story of tortured love. Set in the 1940s, the remoteness of the Seabrook Island setting represents a place apart from the rigid social divides of prewar Charleston, South Carolina.

Beaches are not just another setting where the story happens to unfold. In so many "beach flicks," the sand, sea, surf, and mist are central characters. That's true even when the leading man is someone as wildly famous as Leonardo DiCaprio in his post-*Titanic* heyday. The 2000 adventure drama *The Beach*, filmed on the Thai island of Ko Phi Phi Le, brought so much attention to the island that it had to be closed to the public in 2018. When Maya Bay finally reopened for visitors in 2022, it was with restrictions on the number, and activities, of tourists.

California, the home of Hollywood and the epicenter of world movie production in the 20th century, is unsurprisingly overrepresented on film. With its roughly 840-mile (1,350 km) coastline, the state's beaches often stand in for other parts of the United States, other countries, and even fictional worlds. A recently unearthed map, produced by Paramount Pictures in 1927, illustrates all the locations in California that could pass for foreign locales, from New England (south of San Francisco) to the coast of Spain (from Ventura to Oxnard) to Wales (the Palos Verdes Peninsula).

The beach house from *Beaches*, for example, is actually Cottage #13 at Orange County's Crystal Cove State Park; the sexy beach scene in *The Notebook*—supposedly in South Carolina—was filmed at El Matador State Beach in Malibu; and San Diego's famed beachfront Hotel del Coronado played the part of a Miami hotel in 1959's *Some Like It Hot*, starring Marilyn Monroe. Long Beach's Alamitos Bay stood in for the Chesapeake Bay in the Jack Nicholson and Helen Hunt romantic comedy *As Good as It Gets* (1997), while Seal Beach, one mile (1.6 km) south, passed as Grand Harbor, Michigan, in 2001's *American Pie 2*.

Because of the sheer quantity of movies made in the United States, it's easy to see how the beach and surf culture of the American mid-century lifestyle was exported around the world.

HOSHIZUNA-NO-HAMA BEACH

A beach made of star-shaped sand on one of Japan's most tropical islands

CATEGORY: Unusual   **BEST TIME TO GO:** September through November
WHAT YOU'LL EXPERIENCE: Iriomote-Ishigaki National Park, traditional Okinawan culture, Indo-Pacific Ocean

Japan's lushest, warmest, most tropical region, Okinawa's Yaeyama Islands are home to an unusual beach phenomenon: star sand. Closer to Taiwan than it is to the bigger islands of Japan, Taketomijima is among Japan's southernmost, westernmost inhabited islands. It is also one of the few places in the world with beaches made of tiny, white, star-shaped sand. These spiky grains of calcium carbonate, typically just a few millimeters in size, are actually the exoskeletons of a marine species called foraminifera (*Baculogypsina sphaerulata*), a single-cell organism. This rare creature lives symbiotically among the coral reefs and seagrass of East Asia and in a select few other places on the planet

The water here is shallow and protected, which makes the beach popular with families. The stars are mixed with ordinary grains of sand but become more numerous after storms when they are dislodged from the ocean bottom. They are, therefore, most commonly seen at the tail end of typhoon season, which runs from June through November.

Taketomijima is part of Iriomote-Ishigaki National Park, a subtropical archipelago that is home to both Japan's largest coral reef and its largest mangrove forest, as well as endemic species such as the Iriomote cat and the Sakishima grass lizard. Hoshizuna-no-Hama Beach is a protected area, and it's illegal to take the star sand home.

HISTORY

According to local legend, the star sand is made of the descendants of the North Star and the Southern Cross, which fell into the Okinawa sea. They were ordered to be killed by the god of the sea, who sent a serpent to devour them, leaving their skeletons behind to form the star-sand beach.

The star sand is actually made of the exoskeletons of a marine species called foraminifera.

ITOIGAWA BEACH

A pebble beach on Japan's Jade Coast, where one can find precious gemstones

CATEGORY: Unusual   **BEST TIME TO GO:** July or August for swimming; winter for jade
WHAT YOU'LL EXPERIENCE: Hot springs and *onsens*, UNESCO Global Geopark, Sea of Japan

The beaches of Niigata Prefecture's Jade Coast aren't made of sparkling white sand or lapped by crystalline turquoise waters. Instead, this stretch of Japanese coastline has pebbly shores that have held significance dating back to Japan's ancient Jōmon period (14,500 to 300 B.C.), when it became the center of jade production and trade.

Historically, jade was so prevalent here that locals only collected the best specimens, tossing the rest back into the sea. Once integral to a thriving global trade economy, today Itoigawa is a small city of about 40,000 people. Its history attracts jade enthusiasts and others with an interest in the region's distinctive geology, along with nature lovers drawn to mountains, *onsens* (traditional bathhouses surrounding natural hot springs), and sacred Benten-iwa Rock. The massive landmark rock, created by a submarine volcano, is topped by a shrine dedicated to the sea goddess Ichikishima.

Jade can still be found along Itoigawa's shoreline, designated a UNESCO Global Geopark in 2015, especially after a storm when rough waters churn the seafloor. If one is fortunate enough to find a piece of jade, the nearby Fossa Magna Museum offers a free identification service to authenticate their finding. Hisuien Gardens has a 70-ton (63.5 mt) cobalt jade boulder at its entrance and an impressive Jade Art Museum with elaborate jade carvings.

Benten-iwa Rock, created by an underwater volcano, is home to a shrine dedicated to the sea goddess Ichikishima.

AL FAZAYAH BEACH

An undeveloped coastline of beaches and blowholes near the Yemeni border

CATEGORY: Remote   **BEST TIME TO GO:** July through September
WHAT YOU'LL EXPERIENCE: *Khareef* green landscape, Marneef Cave, Arabian Sea

During the *khareef*, or monsoon rainy season, the vibrant green hillsides in the Salalah region of southern Oman are an unusual sight in the typically arid Arabian Peninsula. It's a dramatically beautiful landscape that remains relatively unvisited, despite an effort to market the coastline as the "Caribbean of the Orient."

The trip to Al Fazayah Beach, 40 miles (64 km) from Salalah, Oman's second largest city, is striking in itself. The long, single-lane gravel road has hairpin turns through coastal mountains and towering headlands, dropping into a stretch of turquoise to deep blue Arabian Sea between the Gulf of Aden and the Persian Gulf. There are a series of beautiful, isolated, undeveloped beaches, including Mughsayl Beach and Shaat Hidden Beach, on either side of Al Fazayah.

The trip to Al Fazayah Beach, which lies near the border with Yemen and is best reached in a four-wheel-drive vehicle, passes two of the coast's best-known sights, Marneef Cave and the Al Mughsayl Blowholes. Here the rocky headlands have been formed and weathered by the sea, which grows turbulent and rough during the khareef, shooting water up to 90 feet (27 m) overhead. This is a stretch of coast where you're likely to be entirely on your own, with the exception of maybe a few nomads and their camels and the occasional adventurous overland camper.

Dramatic rock formations surround the white-sand beach of Al Fazayah.

BA TRAI DAO BEACH

A sliver of a beach against a limestone karst in stunning Lan Ha Bay

CATEGORY: Iconic   BEST TIME TO GO: Year-round, but it's less busy from September through March
WHAT YOU'LL EXPERIENCE: UNESCO Biosphere Reserve, jungle-topped limestone islets, Gulf of Tonkin

Vietnam's expansive Ha Long Bay is perhaps the country's most iconic place, with its emerald waters and thousands of remarkably vertical limestone islands, each capped with lush jungle foliage and plied by junk boats. Within this larger UNESCO World Heritage site, Lan Ha Bay is less visited and comparatively less busy with cruise boat traffic.

These days, the traditional junks mostly carry tourists, who sail to the tiny islands on day trips or overnight cruises. Ba Trai Dao means "Three Peaches" because this islet is one of three tiny limestone islands that, together, resemble lush fruit bobbing in the uncommonly jewel-toned green water of the Gulf of Tonkin.

Because the beach is sheltered by islands, it is ideal for swimming and kayaking. During high tides, the sand is largely underwater, so the beach makes an appearance only two or three hours each day. Many visitors to the beach come as a stop on a tour to Cat Ba National Park, a UNESCO Biosphere Reserve. The park is the only place you can see the wild Cat Ba langur, one of the most critically endangered primates on the planet.

The Cat Ba Archipelago is also home to ancient floating villages, where fishing communities live in boats and floating homes tethered together, some of which offer homestays for an intimate experience of Lan Ha.

Three of Ha Long Bay's more than 1,130 limestone islands surround Ba Trai Dao Beach.

WHITE BEACH

The most famous beach in the Philippines offers a lesson in overtourism.

CATEGORY: Iconic   **BEST TIME TO GO:** November through April (dry season)
WHAT YOU'LL EXPERIENCE: *Paraw* sailboats, White Beach Path, Willy's Rock, Indian Ocean

Since it appeared on the international tourist radar in the 1990s, Boracay has become the Philippines' biggest tourist draw. In a country with 7,641 islands—only about 2,000 of them inhabited—this island stands out for beaches so beautiful they have attracted hordes of visitors (and the haphazard development to accommodate them). In recent years, White Beach, a 2.5-mile-long (4 km) expanse of powdery white sand, has lured more than two million visitors a year to the tiny four-square-mile (10.3 km²) island.

The resulting infrastructure challenges, including an inadequate system for handling the island's sewage, led the president of Philippines to abruptly close Boracay to tourists for a six-month rehabilitation project in 2018. While the island's party atmosphere remains, it's now less crowded. In addition to dismantling a network of illegal sewage pipes and unauthorized waterfront construction, banning its famed fire dancers, and limiting businesses—like bars and henna parlors—from operating on the beach, the government also restricted the number of arrivals.

Along the beach, *paraw* sailboats—traditional Filipino outriggers—continue to ply the clear Pacific waters, offering sunset cruises to visiting beachgoers. The White Beach Path, a coconut palm–shaded pedestrian walk along the beach, has different stations, numbered one, two, and three, that

Willy's Rock is said to be named after a fisherman who sought shelter there during a storm.

ABOVE: **The government now regulates the businesses that line White Beach.**

OPPOSITE: **Sunset highlights the paraw sailboats on the horizon off White Beach.**

are remnants of the boat stations active when people were deposited directly on the beachfront. Today, the path is lined with local businesses of all kinds. Walk until you find your favorite spot, whether it be a massage on the sand beneath a palm tree; the rock formation called Willy's Rock, topped with a statue of the Virgin Mary and surrounded by clear water and white sand; or a stool at one of the beach's waterfront bars.

OTHER BELOVED BEACHES THAT HAVE COMBATED OVERTOURISM

A MAYA BAY, HAT NOPPHARAT THARA-MU KO PHI PHI NATIONAL PARK, THAILAND: Famously depicted in the movie *The Beach* (2000), starring a young Leonardo DiCaprio, this small shoreline—just 49 feet (15 m) wide and 820 feet (250 m) long—surrounded by karst cliffs saw as many as 6,000 visitors per day during its peak of popularity. After a four-year closure to the public, the beach—just south of the resort town of Ao Nang, near Krabi—is now closed for two months each year. When it's open, only 300 people may visit at a time, in about one-hour shifts from 10 a.m. to 4 p.m. In addition, there are restrictions on where boats can anchor, where visitors can walk, and more, in an effort to preserve the area's coral reefs and natural environment.

B SARDINIA, ITALY: Four beaches along the Gulf of Orosei—Cala dei Gabbiani, Cala Biriala, Cala Goloritze, and Cala Mariolu—have imposed a cap of between 250 and 700 visitors a day, based on the size of the beach and that day's crowds. Other beaches on the island have imposed admission charges to fund both services (parking, trails, toilets) and the new, more restrictive regime, which requires would-be beach tourists to book their visit online 72 hours in advance.

C SANTORINI, GREECE: In 2017, this island in the Cyclades group—home to some of the Aegean Sea's most iconic beaches, including Red Beach—limited cruise ship visitors to 8,000 people per day and began encouraging overnight visitors, who tend to spend time in less-touristy parts of the island and offer greater benefit to the local community. The local government also committed to improving the lives of Santorini's mules and donkeys, a significant part of its tourism infrastructure, who trudge up and down the island's steep cliffs where cars aren't able to travel. The reforms include limiting how much weight each animal can carry and increasing the amount of shade and water available to them.

PHRA NANG BEACH

A remote beach with a cave devoted to a fertility princess

CATEGORY: **Unusual**   BEST TIME TO GO: **November through April**
WHAT YOU'LL EXPERIENCE: **Limestone cliffs, long-tail boats, Andaman Sea**

Though it's part of the Thai mainland, the beaches of the Railay (or Rai Leh) Peninsula are only accessible by boat. Just a half hour or so from Krabi, this small boot-shaped peninsula is dominated by imposing limestone cliffs, a dramatic backdrop to its famous white, sandy shores. It's this striking landscape that draws most visitors to Railay. But Phra Nang Beach is notable for another reason: its cave of phalluses.

The Princess Cave at the far end of the beach pays tribute to a princess goddess, Phra Nang, whose spirit is believed to inhabit the cave. The legends surrounding this mythical figure are many and varied. In one, she's a ship-wrecked Indian princess. In an equally moving but more mundane legend, she's the wife of a fisherman who was either lost at sea or abandoned there. In still another story, the female spirit Phra Nang was promised to a sea serpent god or dragon king—or, in some versions, his son—but was in love instead with a local villager. As punishment for disobeying the god/king's demands, her home was turned to stone—a cave where she would live for eternity.

Fishermen seeking safety at sea and abundant harvests, as well as couples struggling with infertility, make offerings to Phra Nang. Her cave is full of incense, food, and other gifts. Most famously, though, the cave is lined with lingams, carved phallic objects that are a symbol of the Hindu god Shiva and

OPPOSITE: **A cave entrance frames beachgoers lazing on Phra Nang Beach.**

PAGES 346-347: **Some visitors rent traditional long-tail boats to travel to Phra Nang Beach.**

are associated with fertility and virility. It's a sacred place for the Thai people and a novelty for tourists (who should still pay the cave and its offerings respect), who lounge along the shoreline, ordering food and Singha beer from the long-tail boats that deliver sustenance to this undeveloped bay.

OTHER NOTABLE BEACHES IN THAILAND

KATA NOI BEACH, PHUKET: Kata Beach is known for its surfable waves. But a mile (1.6 km) south is Kata Noi, a less-bustling beach with great snorkeling that is a short walk to the stunning vistas of Karon Viewpoint.

BANG TAO BEACH, PHUKET: One of the longest beaches in Phuket, this 3.7-mile (6 km) strip of sand is lined with many luxurious resorts.

CHOENG MON BEACH, KOH SAMUI: Swaying palm trees and calm, warm waters make this beach ideal for families who don't want to be tossed around by waves.

SUNRISE BEACH AND SUNSET BEACH, KOH LIPE: While it takes some effort to reach, these lovely beaches, less than a 20-minute walk apart, allow visitors to watch the sun both rise and set on a perfect beach day.

THONG NAI PAN YAI, KO PHA-NGAN: If you travel to the island for the moon festivals, make time to escape the crowds on this white-sand stunner ringed by mountainous rainforest.

PART SIX

OCEANIA

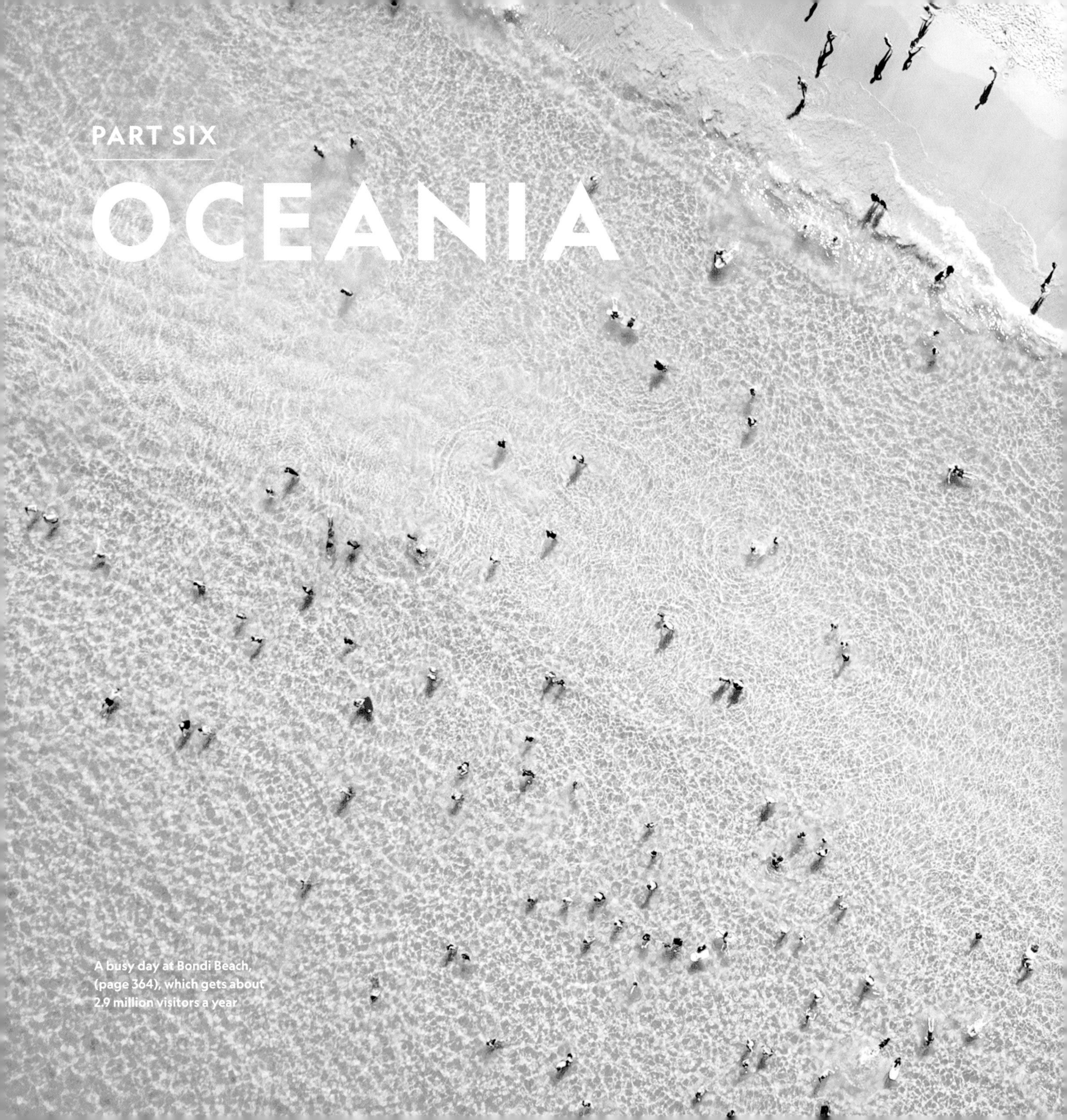

A busy day at Bondi Beach, (page 364), which gets about 2.9 million visitors a year

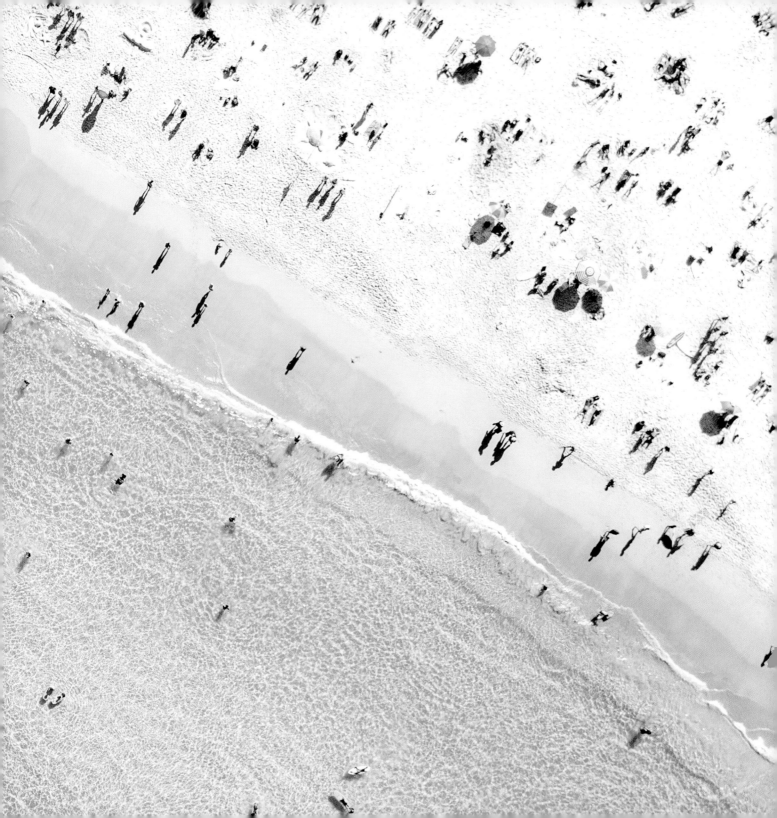

TEREI'A BEACH

A far-flung paradise with bone-white sand and a turquoise lagoon

CATEGORY: Remote   **BEST TIME TO GO:** June through October
WHAT YOU'LL EXPERIENCE: Coconut palms, rays, islets, few people, Pacific Ocean

The westernmost of French Polynesia's Society Islands, Maupiti is a 25-mile (40 km) boat ride from world-famous Bora-Bora. But this tranquil volcanic atoll bears little resemblance to its resort-dominated counterpart. Maupiti is relatively undeveloped and instead oozes with local charm, which is regularly on display at the prettiest spot of all: a thumb-shaped stretch of powdery white sand called Terei'a Beach, which has a bathtub-warm, multihued lagoon.

Most travelers who decide to stay for more than one day stay at the homes of local families or in guesthouses and bungalows, and the hosts provide meals and transport. The first order of business is often a 10-minute drive around the entire island on the one and only coastal road. As it winds around the western edge, visitors catch their first glimpse of Terei'a Beach, a vision of paradise fringed by swaying palm trees. A sparkling turquoise-and-azure lagoon laps the bone-colored shore, and a sense of timelessness hangs on the breeze.

After dropping off luggage and picking up a rental bike, it's time to return to Terei'a to enjoy one of its most enchanting features: the proximity to Motu Auira, a nearby islet with working melon plantations. Beachgoers can wade across the warm, waist-high lagoon to reach the islet (shuffle your feet along the soft bottom, as rays frequent the area). It's also possible to go for a beach

OPPOSITE: Beachgoers can wade through warm, shallow waters from Terei'a Beach to a melon plantation.

PAGES 352-353: The water off Maupiti is typically 81°F (27°C) during the dry season of May through October, making it ideal for snorkeling.

walk, rounding the tip of the thumb and heading south to what's known as Terei'a Varua point. There, you'll find a string of secluded coves and a rock formation shaped like a lizard, which turns up in more than a few local legends.

If you get hungry, there's Chez Mimi, one of two casual restaurants right on the beach that serves freshly grilled fish and hearty sandwiches. After a delicious meal, it's ideal to spend the rest of the day lazing around the beach and watching as the sun dips below the horizon, casting a golden hue over the serene water.

Beyond the beach, visitors enjoy scuba diving with manta rays just offshore, taking boat trips around the lagoon to surrounding coral and sand islets, and hiking through the jungle to the island's highest point. On Saturdays, there's a large gathering out on a nearby islet for Tahitian oven, a giant feast involving traditional foods such as breadfruit, clams, seafood, and pork that are all cooked underground.

To reach the island, you can fly Air Tahiti from Tahiti, Raiatea, or Bora-Bora. Flights are in high demand, so book well in advance. Another option is the 2.5-hour ferry ride on the *Maupiti Express II*, which runs from Bora-Bora to Maupiti (and back) once a week.

FAKARAVA BIOSPHERE RESERVE, FRENCH POLYNESIA

PLAGE DU PK9

White sand and shore snorkeling on a remote coral atoll

CATEGORY: **Remote**   BEST TIME TO GO: **June through October (dry season)**
WHAT YOU'LL EXPERIENCE: **Wall of sharks, UNESCO Biosphere Reserve, Pacific Ocean**

From above, Fakarava Atoll looks like someone drew a near-perfect rectangle on a map of the South Pacific—a thin, elongated line of coral outgrowth surrounds a massive 433-square-mile (1,121 km²) lagoon. But as improbable as Fakarava looks, this 37-mile-long (60 km) by 13-mile-wide (21 km) island, a reef system atop an ancient volcanic seamount, is the second largest atoll in the Tuamotu Islands of French Polynesia.

On this long, narrow, remote atoll, addresses are often given as their distance from Rotoava, the main village. Plage du PK9 is the beach nine kilometers past town down a dirt road. This quintessential French Polynesian beach has excellent snorkeling just offshore and the ruins of a *marae*, or sacred gathering place, a quarter mile (400 m) farther down the road. Locals recommend riding a bike or e-bike from Rotoava and keeping an eye out for falling coconuts.

Fakarava is relatively undeveloped compared to nearby islands like Tahiti and Bora-Bora. Its status as a UNESCO Biosphere Reserve helps protect its spectacular underwater life, which includes colorful coral gardens, mega-schools of tropical fish, and a so-called wall of sharks at the Tumakohua Pass, where the atoll's protected lagoon meets the open ocean. There, it is typical for hundreds of gray reef sharks, the most common species in French Polynesia, to gather to feed, which draws many visitors.

Fakarava's coral atoll is a nature reserve for many rare species of marine life.

CREATURES OF THE INTERTIDAL ZONE

Venture to rocky shores between high and low tide to discover abundant marine life and unique ecosystems.

Where a rocky shore meets a crashing sea between high and low tides, there will be tide pools. And if you've been lucky enough to wander around one of these unusual ecosystems—sometimes called the intertidal zone—you know that it feels a bit like a treasure hunt. Peer into one of these isolated pockets of seawater and you might notice a hermit crab scuttling beneath the surface. Part some seaweed and an otherworldly anemone may be revealed. Glance down at the base of a rock and you may spy a clinging sea star.

If these animals seem bizarre and especially hardy, well, they are. To survive in the intertidal zone is no small feat, as this ever-changing environment requires its denizens to withstand crashing waves, the rising and falling tides, and a rotating cast of wily predators from air, land, and sea. The ebb and flow of the tides, in particular, creates alternating periods of immersion and emersion. At high tide, submerged marine organisms have access to nutrients, oxygen, and protection from predators. But as the tide recedes, the creatures of the intertidal zone are exposed to the elements, with sun, wind, and temperature fluctuations testing their fortitude—not to mention their sudden visibility to predators.

Tide pools are divided into four zones—splash zone, high tide zone, middle tide zone, and low tide zone—based on how high up they are on the beach.

Sally Lightfoot crabs, brightly colored coastal scavengers, are found in the Galápagos Islands.

Only the most robust of all the organisms, such as copepods, lichens, algae, and limpets, can survive in the splash zone with its wild fluctuations in salinity, depleted oxygen levels, and high temperatures. This highest zone on the beach is regularly wetted by waves, ocean spray, and rain, but is rarely if ever submerged. A bit below the splash zone, the high tide zone experiences long periods of exposure to the air and sun at low tide, but becomes fully

Blue mussels are native to Cornwall, England's coast, where they can be found clinging to rocks at low tide.

submerged at high tide. Here you'll find barnacles that close their shells tightly when exposed to air and produce a fast-curing cement-like substance that glues them to rocks.

Continuing down the beach, the middle tide zone is covered and uncovered twice a day. Diversity increases quite a bit here, with anemones, mussels, crabs, and sea stars as regular residents. The low tide zone is exposed only when the tide is unusually low. It supports an array of life, including seaweed, sea urchins, shrimp, snails, and even fish. This zone is not subjected to such large fluctuations in temperature and exposure, making it suitable for more complex and sensitive organisms.

All residents of the intertidal zone have unique adaptations that help them survive in their environment. To avoid drying out or being preyed upon during low tide, mobile organisms like crabs seek refuge in crevices or burrows. When submerged, filter feeders like barnacles and mussels extend specialized appendages into the water to capture plankton and other food sources. And during high tide, some species of sea stars release eggs and sperm into the water to maximize the chances of fertilization.

The lower the tide, the more creatures you're likely to spot. And if you've got a particularly good eye, you may even see a nudibranch. These sluglike creatures are known for their mesmerizing colors and ability to repurpose the weapons of their prey. For example, as a nudibranch consumes a jellyfish, it absorbs its toxins, then later uses them to defend itself from predators. These wondrous creatures can be found in some of the world's best tide pools along the California coast. Other superlative tide pool destinations include the Galápagos Islands, Australia's east coast, and Scotland's Isle of Skye.

Beyond being a riveting place to spend an afternoon—and the inspiration for the wildly popular cartoon *SpongeBob SquarePants*—the intertidal zone plays a crucial role in the overall health of coastal ecosystems. It's a nursery for many marine species, offering shelter and food for juvenile fish and invertebrates. And intertidal habitats contribute to shoreline stabilization, protecting coastal communities from erosion and storms. However, intertidal zones face threats from pollution, overfishing, and habitat destruction. The

impacts of climate change, including sea level rise and warming ocean temperatures, also pose significant challenges to this delicate ecosystem.

To do your part while visiting tide pools, consider bringing an empty bag to collect any trash you find on the beach or in the water. Place your feet on solid rocks and avoid stepping on algae or other sea life. (This will also prevent you from slipping, an easy thing to do in a tide pool environment.) If you pick up a rock, put it back just as you found it, and don't disturb or touch any plants or animals. Collecting intertidal species is illegal in many areas, and should always be avoided as good practice. Leave no trace behind, so others can enjoy these magical tide pools for generations to come.

A Seaweed is exposed when the tide is out along the California Coastal Trail at Redwoods State Park in California.

B The La Jolla tide pools in San Diego, California, offer lots of nooks and crannies for marine life.

C Visitors need to be respectful of the creatures in tide pools so they don't harm any sea life.

D The sun sets over the beach on the Isle of Skye in Scotland.

E The nudibranch, a type of sea slug, absorbs stinging cells from other animals and uses them to defend itself.

F Sea anemones feed in the Channel Islands of California.

G Look at but don't touch the creatures in a tide pool.

SIMPSON HARBOUR BEACH

A scenic harbor precariously situated in a caldera between active volcanoes

CATEGORY: Historical   BEST TIME TO GO: December through March
WHAT YOU'LL EXPERIENCE: The devastated town of Rabaul, hardened lava flows, Pacific Ocean

This muddy volcanic cove in the southwestern Pacific is hardly a place to drop a towel. In fact, the two volcanoes flanking Simpson Harbour could erupt at any time, and have already destroyed the nearby town of Rabaul twice. But a trip to this imperiled shoreline on New Britain, an island of Papua New Guinea, offers a historical and cultural beach experience like no other.

The first time an eruption leveled the town was in 1937, and 263 people were killed. Back then, the island was part of Australia. In 1942, it was bombed and taken over by the Japanese during World War II. After the war, the island became part of the UN Trust Territory of New Guinea (administered by Australia). It was only in 1975, when Papua New Guinea gained its independence, that the island became part of that sovereign nation. Then, in 1994, both Mount Tavurvur and Vulcan Crater erupted, burying Rabaul in volcanic ash and forcing the entire town to evacuate. Thanks to modern technology, this time there were only five casualties.

A few residents, referred to as "the leftovers," returned, but travelers have been drawn in. They walk the bulldozed streets surveying the damage, attend fire dances, feast on the eggs of local megapodes (large, terrestrial birds), scuba dive in the harbor, and paddle out in canoes to check out the southern slopes of Mount Tavurvur, which are caked in hardened lava.

VOLCANIC VACANCY

Just one structure on the main thoroughfare, Mango Avenue, survived the 1994 eruption—the Rabaul Hotel. Photographs on its walls tell the story of this twice-devastated and eventually doomed landscape.

Mount Tavurvur, one of the two volcanoes on the island of New Britain, is also one of the most active in Papua New Guinea.

BONDI BEACH

This beach is an Aussie favorite for its bohemian beach culture and surf scene.

CATEGORY: Iconic   **BEST TIME TO GO: March through April; October through November**
WHAT YOU'LL EXPERIENCE: Coogee Coastal Walk, Bondi Icebergs Swimming Club, Pacific Ocean

In the pantheon of iconic urban beaches, Bondi Beach—in a suburb of Sydney—is as classic as they come. In 1882, the beach was opened to the public, and two years later a tram was built to transport visitors from the city center to the sweeping bayfront. People flocked to the beach, even though "surf bathing"—as beach swimming was called—was banned because it was perceived as indecent. Eventually, the rules were relaxed, and the local Waverley Council built the first surf bathing sheds in about 1903. By 1929, around 60,000 people a day were visiting the beach on a summer weekend, and it is now around 40,000 a day.

The beach's name comes from the Aboriginal word *boondi*, which means "waves breaking on the beach"—a definite nod to the beach's surfable waves. Because of its popularity with both pros and beginner wave riders, the beach currently is divided into zones, with novices, experienced surfers, and swimmers each given their own area. Bondi is a National Surfing Reserve, a designation that aims to promote not only environmental protection of surf spots, but also the culture and economies of surf towns. And Bondi is nothing if not the quintessential surf town.

The beach's history and appeal extend beyond its famous breakers, though. The Bondi Icebergs Swimming Club, with its famous beachside pool—among the most photographed sights in this massive photogenic

OPPOSITE: Lap swimmers enjoy the beachside pool owned by the Bondi Icebergs Swimming Club, which was founded in 1929.

PAGES 366-367: Surfers test the swells at Bondi Beach, which gets consistent quality waves.

country—has been one of the beach's major attractions since it opened in 1929 as a place for lifeguards to maintain their swim practice during the winter months.

Bondi was also among the first places in the world to have beach lifeguards, beginning in 1907. The lifeguard force was formed as more and more people went ocean swimming and got caught up in the beach's currents and rip tides. Similarly, the government of New South Wales began installing shark nets to protect swimmers beginning in 1937. They have been set out every year, from September through April, with the exception of three years during World War II. In recent years, however, the ongoing use of nets at Bondi, and some 50 other beaches between Newcastle and Wollongong in New South Wales, has become controversial because other wildlife, including dolphins and turtles, becomes entangled in them.

Beyond the water, the Bondi to Coogee Coastal Walk is a relatively non-strenuous 3.7-mile (6 km) coastal trail that makes a great day trip. It leads from Bondi all the way to Coogee Beach, passing other gems including Tamarama Beach, Bronte Beach, and Clovelly Beach along the two- to three-hour one-way waterfront walk.

THE IDEAL BEACH SPORT

Once the pastime of royalty, surfing waves now spans the globe from Africa to Antarctica.

There is perhaps no sport or cultural phenomenon more closely associated with the beach than surfing—the pastime of Hawaiian royalty, California beach bums, and countless others around the world. While the modern sport of surfing is relatively new as a global sport (it was popularized in the early 20th century when the United States annexed Hawaii and business interests began promoting tourism to the islands), wave riding dates back thousands of years and to an array of places around the world, including Peru and West Africa.

Surfing came to Hawaii from elsewhere in the Polynesian archipelago, where everyone surfed, from kids to kings, although there were strict rules about who could surf where and how long their surfboards could be.

It was a trio of Hawaiian princes, in California to attend boarding school, who brought surfing to the mainland in 1885. The teenagers had 17-foot-long (5 m) boards made of California redwood, which they paddled into the now famous waves of Santa Cruz, creating an instant sensation among the locals.

Before long, surfing had caught on in California, then spread east to the Atlantic coast, where beaches in both North Carolina and New Jersey claim to be the first East Coast breaks to have been surfed. In Europe, surfers began riding waves in Portugal first, then in France and the United Kingdom. Now, "wave sliding," as it was called in Polynesia, is everywhere from Africa to Antarctica.

Multiple surfers ride a wave at Bondi Beach, which can get incredibly crowded.

WHITEHAVEN BEACH

Sand so fine and white that it swirls like marble in the turquoise water

CATEGORY: Unusual   **BEST TIME TO GO:** May or September
WHAT YOU'LL EXPERIENCE: Hill Inlet, humpback whales, Great Barrier Reef, Pacific Ocean

Off the coast of Queensland, on Australia's eastern seaboard, the Whitsunday Islands (74 in all) are part of one of the country's most revered national parks and the UNESCO Great Barrier Reef World Heritage site. Within this internationally recognized archipelago of coral cays, mangrove forests, lush mountains, and barrier reefs of uncommon biodiversity, Whitehaven Beach is the islands' most celebrated destination.

The sand here is sometimes said to be the whitest in the world, made of 98 percent pure silica beads so tiny and reflective that the grains don't retain the sun's heat. Locals comment that it makes for an especially pleasant—and exfoliating—barefoot stroll. But there's another, even more spectacular reason why this ultrafine, extra-white sand is worth visiting: Whitehaven Beach's spectacular Hill Inlet, where the incoming brilliant blue water meets this exceptional stark-white sand and the two dance with each other in a marble-like swirl of color. It's a gorgeous place for a swim, with water that hovers around 79°F (26°C) year-round.

In addition to the dramatic beauty of the beach, the Whitsundays are a rich environment for wildlife, including blue-bodied soldier crabs, monitor lizards, white-bellied sea eagles, and baby lemon sharks. Stingrays are a notable menace from November through April.

WHALE-WATCHING

The Whitsunday Islands are a World Cetacean Alliance Whale Heritage Area, offering protection to migrating humpback whales, including calves, that are generally seen between July and September.

The turquoise waters, white beaches, and green forests of the Whitsunday Islands are part of the UNESCO Great Barrier Reef World Heritage site.

SHELL BEACH

A beach made entirely of cockleshells in a UNESCO World Heritage area

CATEGORY: Unusual   **BEST TIME TO GO:** April through September
WHAT YOU'LL EXPERIENCE: Francois Peron National Park, Shark Bay World Heritage area, Indian Ocean

Imagine an expansive, stark-white beach (sunglasses recommended) in a narrow U-shaped bay of shockingly clear, intensely blue water. Now imagine that each grain of what you think is sand is actually seashells, trillions of them, so tiny and so prolific they give this unusual place its name: Shell Beach.

The beach is part of the Shark Bay World Heritage area, a geographically and ecologically significant hypersaline bay set within the W formed by two peninsulas and the eastern coast of the mainland. Shell Beach has been an oddity and attraction since the early 1900s, when the beach's abundance of shells was seen mostly as a natural resource to be exploited. The shells were formed into hard-packed blocks and used in construction.

Unlike most other beaches, where the sand is made of seashell remnants, the beach here—part of the roughly 8,500-square-mile (more than 22,000 km²) World Heritage area that includes Francois Peron National Park—is made up entirely of one species, the Fragum cockle. The salinity of Shark Bay, which is twice as salty as typical ocean water, creates an ecosystem where the cockles are virtually without predators or competition and are able to create shell deposits that can reach nearly 33 feet (10 m) deep.

While it's possible to swim here, some find the saltiness of the water unpleasant. Due to the sharpness of the shells, footwear and something thick to lie on are also recommended.

A SEAGRASS SANCTUARY

The surrounding area is home to the largest and richest seagrass beds on the planet, along with some 10,000 dugongs, or sea cows, and a number of other endangered species.

The white shells of the Fragum cockle, which thrive in the salinity of Shark Bay, can appear translucent when held up to light.

LALOMANU BEACH

A beach in a traditional Samoan village, where pristine white sand is lined with *fales*

CATEGORY: Culture   **BEST TIME TO GO:** April through October
WHAT YOU'LL EXPERIENCE: Nu'utele Island, snorkeling and sea kayaking, Pacific Ocean

After hundreds of years of rule by a rotating cast of foreign powers, Samoa won its independence from New Zealand in the 1960s. Despite those centuries of colonial dominance, Samoan culture has remained proudly intact. One sign of that endurance is the *fale* (pronounced fah-lay), a traditional roundhouse that represents "fa'a Samoa"—the Samoan way of life. These simple yet elegant structures are typically built from reeds, wood, or woven palm fronds and have thatched or corrugated tin roofs. They are found on beaches throughout Samoa, including along Lalomanu Beach, where they are operated by locals as affordable, rustic oceanfront accommodations.

Lalomanu, on the south coast of Upolu, Samoa's largest island, is a small village of fewer than 1,000 people. A bit more than an hour from the capital city of Apia, Lalomanu is considered to have one of the most beautiful beaches in the archipelago, with white sand and palms, only interrupted by thatch-roofed fales that look out over a vibrant blue lagoon of exceptionally clear water. Beyond that, visitors can snorkel from shore, and sea kayaking is also popular. The beach offers a spectacular view of the nearby undeveloped island of Nu'utele.

Though the reefs offshore were damaged by a tsunami that swept through in 2009, the beach is as immaculate and breathtaking as ever.

HISTORY

The town of Lalomanu was hit hard by a massive earthquake and resulting tsunami in 2009, but the community has rebuilt. The village's historic landmark, the Congregational Christian Church of Lalomanu, survived because it was built on high ground. It is worth a peek inside to see the intricate detail on the sanctuary's original ceiling.

Brightly colored Samoan *fales* line Lalomanu Beach.

MONURIKI ISLAND

A remote, uninhabited island where a classic beach flick was filmed

CATEGORY: Culture   **BEST TIME TO GO:** May or October (shoulder season)
WHAT YOU'LL EXPERIENCE: Rare iguanas, volcanic cinder cone, Pacific Ocean

The tiny Fijian island of Monuriki is nicknamed "Tom Hanks Island" in honor of its biggest claim to fame: a starring role in the 2000 movie *Cast Away*. Despite being uninhabited, Monuriki (which is also sometimes known as Modriki) has an instantly recognizable profile: a volcanic cinder cone rising from the South Pacific, deep green and palm-studded, fine white sand meeting a turquoise lagoon. Its most notable resident, beyond "Wilson"—the volleyball companion from the movie, a prop for visiting film buffs left by tour guides on what has been dubbed Castaway Island Beach—is the rare Fijian crested iguana, which is the focus of intense conservation efforts.

Like so much of what was seen on-screen, the island appears almost too good to be true. One has to wonder how many immaculate tropical islands the *Cast Away* production team had to visit before finding this almost impossibly picturesque setting.

But beyond the novelty of a movie star beach, Monuriki is a dazzling place. Part of the Mamanuca Islands, it is just about an hour by boat from the main Fijian island of Viti Levu. Unsurprisingly, Monuriki has become a popular day trip from Nadi and the other 20 Mamanuca Islands. Because Monuriki is entirely undeveloped, visitors typically spend a couple of leisurely hours there swimming, climbing palm trees, and taking pictures with a volleyball.

WHICH CASTAWAY?

Somewhat confusingly, a nearby island— privately owned and operated as a resort— has been renamed Castaway (formerly Qalito), causing some tourists to mistake the two.

Visitors can play castaway on the pristine beaches of Monuriki.

HOT WATER BEACH

A steaming beach where subterranean hot springs are turned into natural hot tubs

CATEGORY: **Unusual**   BEST TIME TO GO: **Year-round**
WHAT YOU'LL EXPERIENCE: **Turbulent ocean, geothermal activity, Pacific Ocean**

There's a beach about 109 miles (175 km) from Auckland at the northeast tip of the Coromandel Peninsula in New Zealand where each day a swarm of people appear for two hours before and after low tide. They've come to Hot Water Beach for an unusual seaside attraction: a steaming expanse of exposed sand that's warm to the touch and scorchingly hot—147°F (64°C)—just beneath the surface. The phenomena is the result of subterranean hot springs; there are two fissures at the beach from which this naturally heated water rises almost to the surface.

When the tide is right, a combination of dedicated locals and visitors work hurriedly to dig human-size holes in the sand—temporary hot tubs for soaking beside the roaring sea. The temperature of the water is hottest closest to the spring, so visitors carefully select the right location for a comfortable bath. For those who forget their shovel or spade, local shops offer them for rent. The ocean here is wild and its rip currents are dangerous. Visitors to the beach should beware of turning their back on the waves as they excavate.

If you want to swim on the Coromandel Peninsula, visit nearby Cathedral Cove Beach. Known as Te Whanganui-o-Hei in the local Indigenous language, the shore is accessible by boat, kayak, or water taxi (the walking path is currently closed). It is home to a towering stone arch that overhangs the sand, and 'Te Hoho, a sea-weathered pinnacle of rock that's a local landmark.

Visitors soak in the hot tubs that they dug on Hot Water Beach.

GEOTHERMAL AND HOT SPRINGS BEACHES

Hot springs are found all over the planet, from the mountains to the desert. The naturally heated water, warmed by Earth's geothermal energy, has been enjoyed by humans for millennia for its novelty and healing properties. Some hot springs flow directly into the sea or emerge from beneath it to warm frigid ocean water enough to make it swimmable. Here are a few noteworthy hot springs beaches around the globe.

PENDULUM COVE, DECEPTION ISLAND, ANTARCTICA: The black-sand beach at Pendulum Cove on Deception Island, a volcanic caldera just off Antarctica, is a popular stop on tourist expeditions to the South Pole. Visitors are shuttled ashore to the horseshoe-shaped, glacier-capped island, where they strip from their layers and throw themselves into Antarctic water warmed—albeit only to about 70°F (21°C)—by undersea fumaroles (openings in Earth's crust that release steam).

LE FUMAROLE BEACH, ISCHIA, ITALY: On the Italian island of Ischia, off the coast of Naples, the sand at Le Fumarole Beach is heated by subterranean steam vents. Here, the sand can become so hot in places that it has been used by locals to cook food.

NAUTHÓLSVÍK GEOTHERMAL BEACH, REYKJAVÍK, ICELAND: While human-made beaches in big cities around world are nothing new, the Nauthólsvík Geothermal Beach in Reykjavík stands alone as a geothermal water-fed hot spring lagoon with an artificially sandy shore. This engineered seaside hot spring forces warm geothermal water to mingle with Iceland's chilly sea, bringing the lagoon's water temperature up to a swimmable mid-60s Fahrenheit (nearly 20°C) during the summer months.

Steam rises from the water of Pendulum Cove on Deception Island.

KOEKOHE BEACH

A beach with massive boulders that have meaning to the Indigenous Māori

CATEGORY: Historical   **BEST TIME TO GO:** December through February
WHAT YOU'LL EXPERIENCE: Rare endemic species, 65-million-year-old rock formations, Pacific Ocean

An hour north of Dunedin, on the Otago coast of New Zealand's South Island, Koekohe Beach is known for the more than 70 massive, improbably round boulders strewn over the sand. The unusual rocks, which are called concretions, can measure more than six feet (2 m) in diameter and weigh several tons. They're made of a naturally occurring mineral "cement" of sedimentary rock, millions of years old, and tougher than the earth that surrounds them. Ocean erosion carves away at the cliffs and beach, leaving the boulders intact.

The beach is near the historic Māori fishing village of Moeraki, where the boulders have a deeper meaning. Koekohe is believed to be among the first places that the Māori landed when they arrived in New Zealand sometime between A.D. 1250 and 1300. According to legend, the Moeraki Boulders (called *Te Kaihīnaki* in the Indigenous language) are not simply rocks, but the remains of precious supplies—eel baskets, gourds, and sweet potatoes—lost when a sailing canoe, *Āraiteuru*, capsized and washed ashore, forming Shag Point.

After years of boulders being pilfered from the beach, Koekohe is now protected by the Moeraki Boulders Scenic Reserve, which also offers sanctuary to local wildlife, including yellow-eyed penguins (*hoiho*), which are among the rarest penguin species in the world; New Zealand sea lions, known as *rāpoka*; and Hector's dolphins.

OPPOSITE: Sunrise glints off the Moeraki Boulders as the tide rushes in.

PAGES 384-385: The landmark of Vase Rock on Xiao Liuqiu in Taiwan marks a beach ideal for snorkeling with sea turtles.

For maximum boulder-viewing opportunities, it's best to visit at low tide, when fewer of the ancient stones are submerged. But some visitors argue that visiting mid-tide, when the giant spheres appear to float on the water or are being splashed by waves, makes for an even more intriguing sight.

OTHER BEACHES WITH UNUSUAL ROCK FORMATIONS

PLAYA DEL AMOR, MARIETA ISLANDS, MEXICO: On an island 22 miles (35 km) from Puerto Vallarta in the Gulf of Mexico, this sinkhole beach—said to be a hideaway for lovers—is part of Marieta Islands National Park, a conservation effort spearheaded by Jacques Cousteau. Essentially an underground beach, Playa del Amor is also known as Hidden Beach. It's surrounded by overhanging rock walls that open to a near circular skylight above. The only way in is through a water tunnel.

PLAYA DE LAS CATEDRALES, RIBADEO, SPAIN: This Galician natural monument that's officially known as Praia de Augas Santas (Beach of the Holy Waters) is a series of tall stone arches—some 90 feet (27 m) high—towering over a sandy beach. The Gothic cathedral-like arches are best experienced at low tide. Visitors are limited to 5,000 people per day.

XIAO LIUQIU, TAIWAN: This small coral island off the coast of Taiwan is known for its rock formations, including the nearly 30-foot-tall (9 m) coral-limestone Vase Rock. Eroded at its base by waves from the South China Sea, the top-heavy formation is covered with vegetation, making it look like a vase sprouting greenery. There's a small beach onshore, as well as Zhongao Beach and Secret Beach nearby.

BEACH CONSERVATION

Among the myriad ways human activity, development, and climate change affect the planet, the disappearance and diminishing of beaches are among the most visible. Like the figurative canary in the coal mine, ocean beaches—where the sea and the land meet—are often an early and concerning indicator of the perils of our changing world.

Rising sea levels, coastal flooding, and erosion are already taking a toll on coastal communities from Miami Beach, a low-lying barrier island, to the central Pacific island nation of Kiribati, which is considered to be among the countries most at risk from climate change.

In response, local and national governments are investing in strategies to save their coastlines. And the international community, through the United Nations Intergovernmental Panel on Climate Change (IPCC), among other organizations, is coordinating a global effort to address the threat.

Increasingly, conservation efforts are turning to coastal restoration to create a natural buffer of wetlands, sand dunes, and wild coastal habitats between rising oceans and communities. Often, this means removing structures—including seawalls, boardwalks, piers, and other fixed human development—which alters how people interact with the shoreline. Embracing these changes can be challenging, especially because waterfront real estate is often considered the most valuable, but it is one of the best long-term strategies for preserving beaches and coastal ecosystems, according to scientists.

Planting mangroves helps stabilize the shoreline through the plants' ability to reduce the force of waves, capture sediment, and build soil.

PLANET OR PLASTIC?

In May 2018, National Geographic launched its Planet or Plastic? campaign, a multiyear effort to raise awareness about the global plastic crisis. A few fast plastic facts for you:

- Half of all plastics ever manufactured have been made in the last 20 years, and nearly a million plastic bottles are sold every minute around the world.

- More than 40 percent of plastic is used once and then discarded, and 6.3 billion tons (5.7 billion mt) of plastic fill our landfills, landscapes, and oceans.

- Every year, about eight million tons (7.3 million mt) of plastic waste escape into the oceans from coastal nations. That's the equivalent of five garbage bags full of trash on every foot of coastline around the world.

- Plastic takes nearly 400 years to degrade.

Beachgoers don't need to wait for an organized cleanup to remove litter and help protect marine ecosystems.

Not sure where to begin? Here are seven guidelines to get you started on your conservation journey.

1 VOTE: This is an easy—and important—one. Vote for politicians who champion conservation and let them (and their opponents) know why. Be vocal. For as much good as we're doing individually, we need lawmakers to back it up on a global level.

2 SUPPORT SCIENCE: Misinformation and lack of funding are making scientific research difficult, right when we need it most. Whether a grassroots project at your local beach, organizations looking at the larger picture, or solution-focused companies, you can provide support by donating your time, volunteering your individual expertise, or backing them financially. Get involved.

3 REALIZE IMPACT STARTS AT HOME: Being aware of stormwater runoff, and how pollution in watersheds affects the beaches downstream, goes a long way—even if you live nowhere near a beach. This includes minimizing the use of fertilizers, which contribute to algae blooms and so-called dead zones offshore, maintaining septic systems, and properly disposing of pet waste and household trash.

4 LEAVE NO TRACE: At the beach, embracing a leave-no-trace ethos protects these ecosystems and makes them more enjoyable places to spend time. Using reusable containers for your picnic lunch and avoiding single-use packaging helps minimize trash inadvertently finding its way to the beach and ocean, while also protecting marine species from ingesting or entangling themselves in trash. Taking care to walk on established pathways to and from the beach, to avoid trampling on established shore grasses and plant life, helps protect against erosion.

5 USE SUNSCREEN SMARTS: Sunscreens can contain chemicals such as oxybenzone that are highly toxic to juvenile corals and other marine life. Applying a reef-friendly sunscreen or wearing UPF clothing instead helps preserve the coral systems integral to beaches around the world.

6 VOLUNTEER: For those who want to go beyond their footprint to volunteer for beach cleanups and advocate for beach-friendly policies, seek out conservation organizations in your region.

7 REMEMBER THAT PLASTIC IS NOT SO FANTASTIC: Be mindful of the amount of plastic you use in your everyday life and take active steps to reduce it. You can do this at the beach by bringing reusable water bottles, as well as multiuse utensils, instead of plastic, that you can take home and wash. (That means avoiding plastic straws, too!) It's that simple—and that effective.

DESTINATIONS BY LOCATION

ACKNOWLEDGMENTS

As sea levels rise, ocean water temperatures increase, and beaches face other human-caused threats, those of us who love the world's shorelines owe our gratitude to the scientists and advocates working to protect these irreplaceable places. This includes researchers studying ways to decrease erosion, save coral reefs, and confront global climate change, as well as the advocates who work to turn that research into action. These devoted coastal and environmental stewards are not only protecting our coastlines for us but for future generations.

Ashley would like to thank her dad for the brilliant idea to get scuba certified together when she was a kid, and her mom—who was terrified of water and never learned to swim—for allowing it. She deeply appreciates each and every friend who accompanied her on a beach trip (Freda included), and also her boyfriend, Jonah Page, who constantly scavenges beaches for the best rocks and driftwood. Finally, she'd like to thank her dog, Osa, for demanding beach trips on a daily basis and looking adorable while running in the sand.

Freda's love for beaches, waterways, and shores comes from her dad, an early surfer, longtime sailor, tide pool explorer, and perpetual adventurer. For that, and much else, she is forever grateful. It was her kids, Roxie and Felix, with their innate curiosity and joyful appreciation of sand and water, that made beaches places of wonder. Without her husband, Tim Stelloh, this book could not have happened. Because someone has to watch the kids while Freda is lounging on the beach.

Special thanks to the team at Indelible Editions, including Dinah Dunn and Jen Quinn, for believing in this book and bringing it to life. And thank you to the team at National Geographic Books, including Allyson Johnson, Elisa Gibson, Adrian Coakley, Anne LeongSon, and Becca Saltzman, for giving this book a home.

ABOUT THE AUTHORS

A lifelong beach enthusiast, FREDA MOON is a California-based travel journalist who has written for the *New York Times*, *National Geographic Traveler*, *AFAR*, and *Sunset*, among others. She also co-wrote *Cabin Porn: Inside* and contributed to Taschen's *The New York Times* books, including *Explorer: Mountains, Deserts & Plains*, several *36 Hours* compilations, and *The Cultured Traveler*. Her work has appeared in *The Best American Travel Writing* anthology, and she has won both the Society of American Travel Writers Foundation's Lowell Thomas Travel Journalism Award and multiple North American Travel Journalists Association awards. She lives in a vintage trawler in the San Francisco Bay with her family.

ASHLEY HARRELL is a journalist who writes about travel, wildlife, and the sea. She's reported from 17 countries, co-authored more than 50 guidebooks, and works at *SFGATE* covering California's national parks. Her work has appeared in outlets such as *National Geographic*, the *Los Angeles Times*, and the *Telegraph*, and her story about a killer Costa Rica rodeo bull was a finalist for the Livingston Award for Young Journalists. When not on assignment, you'll find her jumping on trampolines, scuba diving, and taking photos of wild animals. She lives with her boyfriend and dog in Humboldt County, California.

ILLUSTRATIONS CREDITS

Front cover, 1, Denis Belitsky/Shutterstock; 2-3, Jenny Sturm/Shutterstock; 4-5, marako85/Adobe Stock Photo; 7, 8-9, Ray Collins; 11, Freda Moon/The New York Times/Redux; 12, Susan Vineyard/Adobe Stock Photo; 14, SeanPavonePhoto/Adobe Stock Photo; 15, Tom Norring/Danita Delimont/Adobe Stock Photo; 17, ggfoto/Adobe Stock Photo; 18a, Alexandree/Shutterstock; 18b, ggfoto/Adobe Stock Photo; 18c, Chris Rohner/500px/Getty Images; 18d, H-Media/Adobe Stock Photo; 18e, Stefano Dalle Luche/Alamy Stock Photo; 18f, Jason Busa/Shutterstock; 18g, Raymond Choong/Shutterstock; 18h, proslgn/Adobe Stock Photo; 18i, Michele/Adobe Stock photo; 20-21, Jessica/Adobe Stock Photo; 23, Cannon Photography LLC/Alamy Stock Photo; 24-25, Simon Dannhauer/Alamy Stock Photo; 27, Andy Troy/Shutterstock; 28a, Hemis/Alamy Stock Photo; 28b, Gail Johnson/Shutterstock; 28c, Chiyacat/Shutterstock; 31, Nejron Photo/Shutterstock; 32, BlueOrange Studio/Adobe Stock Photo; 34, Elizabeth Caron/Shutterstock; 35, Kaspars/Adobe Stock Photo; 37, Giacomo/Adobe Stock Photo; 39, Henrry Josue Trejo Gomez/Shutterstock; 41, Design Pics Inc/Alamy Stock Photo; 42, Tomas Kulaja/Shutterstock; 44, chrisdonaldsonphotography/Shutterstock; 45, Caron Palmer/Shutterstock; 47, Ronnie Chua/Shutterstock; 49, REDA&CO/Getty Images; 50-51, KikoStock/Shutterstock; 53, JUAN CARLOS MUNOZ/Adobe Stock Photo; 54-55, Thorsten Spoerlein/Shutterstock; 57, John Michaels/Alamy Stock Photo; 58-59, Pete Niesen/Alamy Stock Photo; 61, Warren H/Shutterstock; 63, H-Media/Adobe Stock Photo; 64a, Cavan Images/Alamy Stock Photo; 64b, J Steele/Shutterstock; 64c, Buzz Pictures/Alamy Stock Photo; 65d, ANDREI/Adobe Stock Photo; 65e, Nikita M production/Shutterstock; 67, mogamju/Adobe Stock Photo; 68-69, Rodrigo Friscione/Getty Images; 71, Dan Oldenburg/Alamy Stock Photo; 73, Matt Gush/Shutterstock; 74-75, Ldurate/Shutterstock; 77, Curioso.Photography/Shutterstock; 78-79, Marek Poplawski/Shutterstock; 81, Darryl Brooks/Shutterstock; 82-83, Tony Florio/Alamy Stock Photo; 85, Moose1/Stockimo/Alamy Stock Photo; 86-87, Design Pics Inc/Alamy Stock Photo; 89, Marc Guitard/Getty Images; 91, fokke baarssen/Shutterstock; 92-93, BlueOrange Studio/Shutterstock; 95, GeoStills/Alamy Stock Photo; 96, Paper and Lens Co/Shutterstock; 98a, Jim Lundgren/Stockimo/Alamy Stock Photo; 98b, Alisha Bube/Shutterstock; 98c, Sipa USA/Alamy Stock Photo; 99, Cosmo Condina North America/Alamy Stock Photo; 101, Clarence Holmes Photography/Alamy Stock Photo; 102-103, Patrick F Infante/Shutterstock; 105, Stream Skins/Adobe Stock Photo; 107, Joseph Sohm/Shutterstock; 108, travelview/Adobe Stock Photo; 110, James Shin/Adobe Stock Photo; 111, McKayla Chandler/Shutterstock; 113, Earth Pixel LLC/Adobe Stock Photo; 114, Laura Grier/Robert Harding; 116a, Christian Mueller/Shutterstock; 116b, creativefamily/Adobe Stock Photo; 116c, Yurok Aleksandrovich/Adobe Stock Photo; 116d, FilippoBacci/Getty Images; 116e, Martin Valigursky/Adobe Stock Photo; 117f, Rui/Adobe Stock Photo; 117g, QualityMaster/Shutterstock; 119, Chris Martin/Alamy Stock Photo; 121, Hana Sladeckova/Alamy Stock Photo; 122-123, ggfoto/Adobe Stock Photo; 125, Russ Bishop/Alamy Stock Photo; 126-127, Wirestock, Inc./Alamy Stock Photo; 129, Laura Grier/Robert Harding; 131, Bob Pool/Shutterstock; 132-133, Bob Pool/Shutterstock; 135, Jason Busa/Shutterstock; 136a, Marla Holde/Alamy Stock Photo; 136b, IrinaK/Shutterstock; 136c, John/Adobe Stock Photo; 136d, Martin Thomas Photography/Alamy Stock Photo; 136e, MelissaMN/Adobe Stock Photo; 136f, Joe Simoy/Shutterstock; 138-139, Jefferson Bernardes/Shutterstock; 141, JHVEPhoto/Shutterstock; 142, PTZ Pictures/Adobe

Stock Photo; 144, Alexandree/Shutterstock; 145, Atosan/Shutterstock; 147, Jo/Adobe Stock Photo; 149, Zenobillis/Alamy Stock Photo; 151, Karol Kozlowski/Robert Harding; 152-153, Karol Kozlowski Premium RM Collection/Alamy Stock Photo; 155, Christian Peters/Alamy Stock Photo; 157, aure50/Alamy Stock Photo; 158a, John/Alamy Stock Photo; 158b, monticellllo/Alamy Stock Photo; 158c, GRP Imagery/Alamy Stock Photo; 159d, Visions from Earth/Alamy Stock Photo; 159e, Henn Photography/Cavan Images; 161, Michele/Adobe Stock Photo; 163, Riccardo Orizio/Shutterstock; 164, Leonardo/Adobe Stock Photo; 166a, Hemis/Alamy Stock Photo; 166b, Luciano Albano/Shutterstock; 166c, Rick Neves/Adobe Stock Photo; 167, reubergd/Adobe Stock Photo; 169, lazyllama/Adobe Stock Photo; 171, James Morgan/Robert Harding; 172-173, schame87/Adobe Stock Photo; 175, THEPALMER/Getty Images; 176a, Stanley Cabigas/Alamy Stock Photo; 176b, Hafizussalam bin Sulaiman/Shutterstock; 176c, Ocaskay Mark/Shutterstock; 176d, Brent Hofacker/Adobe Stock Photo; 176e, godongphoto/Shutterstock; 178, Robert Briggs/Shutterstock; 179b, Bryce/Adobe Stock Photo; 179c, hadasit/Shutterstock; 181, Jon Arnold Images Ltd/Alamy Stock Photo; 182-183, Fotos 593/Adobe Stock Photo; 185, Giedriius/Shutterstock; 187, 55° Photography/Adobe Stock Photo; 188-189, Aliaksandr Antanovich/Shutterstock; 191, Jim/Adobe Stock Photo; 193, Liam/Adobe Stock Photo; 195, allouphoto/Adobe Stock Photo; 197, tolobalguer.com/Shutterstock; 199, Polonio Video /Adobe Stock Photo; 201, Guido Nicora/Shutterstock; 203, Stefano Dalle Luche/Alamy Stock Photo; 205, Eve Bocek/Shutterstock; 206a, Only France/Alamy Stock Photo; 206b, Eva Bocek/Shutterstock; 206c, Tristan Deschamps/Alamy Stock Photo; 207, Wilfried Feder/Westend61/Alamy Stock Photo; 209, janoka82/Adobe Stock Photo; 210-211, Janos Gaspar/Alamy Stock Photo; 213, Ron Niebrugge/Alamy Stock Photo; 214a, Robert Harding Video/Shutterstock; 214b, EB Adventure Photography/Shutterstock; 214c, daliu/Adobe Stock Photo; 215d, nomadkate/Shutterstock; 215e, Terence Waeland/Alamy Stock Photo; 217, Benno Hoff/Shutterstock; 219, Pawel Kazmierczak/Shutterstock; 221, Ashley Cooper pics/Alamy Stock Photo; 222-223, Georgis Tsichlis/Shutterstock; 225, Roberto Moiola/Sysaworld/Getty Images; 227, Dreamer4787/Shutterstock; 229, AlexAnton/Shutterstock; 230-231, zevana/Shutterstock; 233, ploosy/Adobe Stock Photo; 235, ARoxoPT/Shutterstock; 237, Marcel/Adobe Stock Photo; 238, Smit/Shutterstock; 240, Maridav/Adobe Stock Photo; 241, Filip Fuxa/Shutterstock; 243, Andrew Mayovskyy/Shutterstock; 245, Valentin Weinhäupl/Westend61/Alamy Stock Photo; 246a, Andrew Mayovskyy/Shutterstock; 246b, Foto 4440/Shutterstock; 246c, RuslanKphoto/Adobe Stock Photo; 246d, d3_plus D.Naruse @ Japan/Getty Images; 246e, Anthony Brown/Adobe Stock Photo; 247, Jonas Tufvesson/Shutterstock; 248-249, fokke baarssen/Shutterstock; 251, Hemis/Alamy Stock Photo; 252-253, gabrielsarabando/Shutterstock; 255, simo/Alamy Stock Photo; 256-257, Solodova Eva/Shutterstock; 259, Steffen/Adobe Stock Photo; 261, idfied/Shutterstock; 263, Stephen Gichuru/Shutterstock; 265, Cavan Images/Alamy Stock Photo; 266-267, Dominyk Lever/Shutterstock; 269, Szymon Barylski/Shutterstock; 271, Radek Borovka/Shutterstock; 273, Pete Hendley/Alamy Stock Photo; 274a, Westend61 GmbH/Alamy Stock Photo; 274b, frantisek hojdysz/Adobe Stock Photo; 274c, Christopher Moswitzer/Shutterstock; 275d, Rui Leca/Shutterstock; 275e, Irina Naoumova/Alamy Stock Photo; 277, Lucas/Adobe Stock Photo; 279, vkilikov/Shutterstock; 281, Daniel Zanchi/Amazing Aerial Agency; 283, Chris Rohner/500px/Getty Images; 285, davidf/Getty Images; 286a, mahatma/Adobe Stock Photo; 286b, Southern Creative/Adobe Stock Photo; 286c, Gonzales Photo/Alamy Stock Photo; 287d, Nick Bywater/Alamy Stock Photo; 287e, In These Moments Studio/Alamy Stock Photo; 289, Lee-Anne Robertson/Shutterstock; 290a, Piman Khrutmuang/Adobe Stock Photo; 290b, DRNO/Alamy Stock Photo; 290c, Cyndi Monaghan/Getty Images; 290d, Hemis/Alamy Stock Photo; 290e, Fireflywishes/Stockimo Alamy Stock Photo; 291f, Mario

Since 1888, the National Geographic Society has funded more than 14,000 research, conservation, education, and storytelling projects around the world. National Geographic Partners distributes a portion of the funds it receives from your purchase to National Geographic Society to support programs including the conservation of animals and their habitats.

National Geographic Partners, LLC
1145 17th Street NW
Washington, DC 20036-4688 USA

Get closer to National Geographic Explorers and photographers, and connect with our global community. Join us today at nationalgeographic.org/joinus

For rights or permissions inquiries, please contact National Geographic Books
Subsidiary Rights: bookrights@natgeo.com

Produced by Indelible Editions

INDELIBLE
EDITIONS

ISBN: 978-1-4262-2390-7

Printed in South Korea

24/QPSK/1

The information in this book has been carefully checked and to the best of our knowledge is accurate. However, details are subject to change, and the publisher cannot be responsible for such changes, or for errors or omissions. Assessments of sites, hotels, and restaurants are based on the author's subjective opinions, which do not necessarily reflect the publisher's opinion.

HUNDREDS OF ADVENTURES TO EXPLORE

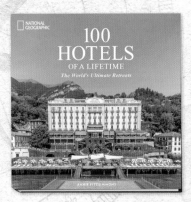

NATIONAL GEOGRAPHIC

100 HOTELS OF A LIFETIME

The World's Ultimate Retreats

ANNIE FITZSIMMONS

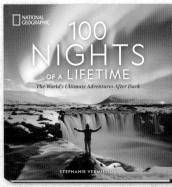

NATIONAL GEOGRAPHIC

100 NIGHTS OF A LIFETIME

The World's Ultimate Adventures After Dark

STEPHANIE VERMILLION

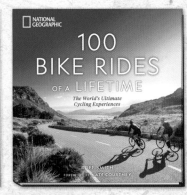

NATIONAL GEOGRAPHIC

100 BIKE RIDES OF A LIFETIME

The World's Ultimate Cycling Experiences

ROFF SMITH

FOREWORD BY KATE COURTNEY

NATIONAL GEOGRAPHIC

100 DISNEY ADVENTURES OF A LIFETIME

Magical Experiences From Around the World

MARCY CARRIKER SMOTHERS

FOREWORD BY JOE ROHDE

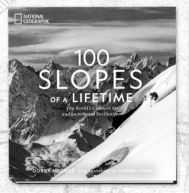

NATIONAL GEOGRAPHIC

100 SLOPES OF A LIFETIME

The World's Ultimate Ski and Snowboard Destinations

GORDY MEGROZ WITH A FOREWORD BY LINDSEY VONN

NATIONAL GEOGRAPHIC

100 DIVES OF A LIFETIME

The World's Ultimate Underwater Destinations

NATIONAL GEOGRAPHIC

100 HIKES OF A LIFETIME

The World's Ultimate Scenic Trails